ALSO BY WILL SCHWALBE

The End of Your Life Book Club

Send
(with David Shipley)

BOOKS *for Living*

BOOKS *for Living*

WILL SCHWALBE

ALFRED A. KNOPF

New York

2017

THIS IS A BORZOI BOOK
PUBLISHED BY ALFRED A. KNOPF

Copyright © 2016 by Will Schwalbe

www.aaknopf.com

Knopf, Borzoi Books, and the colophon are registered trademarks
of Penguin Random House LLC.

Owing to limitations of space, all acknowledgments
for permissions to reprint previously published material
may be found at the end of the volume.

Library of Congress Cataloging in Publication Control Number:
2016026088

ISBN 978-0-385-35354-0 (hardcover) | ISBN 978-0-385-35355-7 (ebook)

Jacket design by Carol Devine Carson and Chip Kidd

Manufactured in the United States of America
First Edition

For David Cheng
And for Andy Brimmer and Tom Molner

"A reader lives a thousand lives before he dies," said Jojen. "The man who never reads lives only one."

—GEORGE. R. R. MARTIN, *A Dance with Dragons*

Contents

BOOKS *for Living*

Introduction

FROM TIME TO TIME I have a terrifying dream. I call it the Reader's Nightmare.

I'm in a busy airport, and they've announced my flight. There is an epic walk to the gate, and I know I have only a few minutes before they will close the door to the jetway and my plane will leave without me. Suddenly, I realize that I don't have a book to read on the flight. Not one single book. I spin around, my eyes searching frantically for a bookstore. I see none. I run through the airport, past the duty-free counters selling liquor and perfume, past the luggage stores and fashion boutiques, past the place that offers neck massage. Still, I can't find an airport bookstore. Now, over the loudspeakers, comes the final call for my flight. "Flight ninety-seven to Perth is ready for departure. All passengers must be on board at this time." They even call me by name. Panic sets in as I realize that I am almost certainly going to miss my flight. But the idea of hours on a plane without a book? Intolerable. So I run and run, searching for that bookstore—or at least a newsstand with a rack of paperbacks. I can't find a single book anywhere in the airport. I start to scream.

Then I wake up.

I don't have this dream about food or television or movies or music. My unconscious is largely untroubled by the idea of spending hours in a metal tube hurtling through the sky without something to eat or a program to watch or tunes in my ears. It's the thought of being bookless for hours that jolts me awake in a cold sweat.

Throughout my life I've looked to books for all sorts of reasons: to comfort me, to amuse me, to distract me, and to educate me. But just because you know that you can find anything you need in a book doesn't mean you can easily find your way to the right book at the right time, the one that tells you what you need to know or feel when you need to know or feel it.

A few years ago, I wrote a book about the books I read with my mother when she was dying of pancreatic cancer. During this time we read casually, promiscuously, and whimsically, allowing one book to lead us to the next. We read books we were given and books that had sat on our shelves for decades, waiting to be noticed; books we had stumbled across, and books we had chosen to reread simply because we felt like it. Were we looking for anything in particular? Usually not. At times, the books gave us something to talk about when we wanted to talk about anything rather than her illness. But they also gave us a way to talk about subjects that were too painful to address directly. They helped guide and prompt our conversations, so that I could learn as much as I could from my mother while she was still here to teach me.

At other times throughout my life, though, I've felt a very specific need and have searched for a book to answer it. It hasn't always been easy to find the right book. Sure, when that burning need was to learn how to make a pineapple upside-down cake, I turned to *The Cake Bible*. Or when it was a need to find a place to eat in Chicago, the *Zagat* guide. Or when I wanted to self-diagnose that angry rash, to the *Mayo Clinic Family Health Book*. More and more, when I need this kind of information, my first line of attack isn't a book at all—it's the Internet, or social media, where I quiz the ubiquitous "hive mind" to find, say, good Malaysian food near Union Square.

There are, however, questions that the Internet and the hive mind are spectacularly unable to answer to my satisfaction. These are the big ones, the ones that writers have been tackling for thousands of years: the problem of pain, meaning, purpose, happiness. Questions about how to live your life. Yes, the Internet tries to help—inasmuch as any inanimate thing can be said to try to do anything. There are digital video channels devoted to streaming inspirational speeches from conferences in which people package insight into brief uplifting lectures—many with a compelling hook and some memorable stories. But the best of these are often simply digests of— or advertisements for—a book that the presenter has written or is currently working on. Authors have always given lectures: there's nothing new in that. And readers, after hearing such speeches, have craved the books that go with them, so that they could explore the topics in greater depth and engage with them more fully—working through the arguments at their own pace, skipping, savoring, and pondering.

Unlike most of these inspirational speeches, even the best of which tend to be largely self-referential, most good books are not tackling big questions in isolation. Great authors have been engaged in a dialogue with one another that stretches back for millennia. People who write books generally read books, and most books carry with them traces of some of the hundreds or thousands of books the writer read before attempting the one at hand.

And that's also why books can echo for centuries into the future. Even a book read by only a dozen people can have a massive effect if one of those readers goes on to write a book read by millions. British writer Henry Green (real name: Henry Vincent Yorke) never sold more than a few thousand copies of any of his novels, and most of his books sold far fewer than that. But the writers influenced by Green include Sebastian Faulks (whose *Birdsong* is one of the bestselling and most beloved British novels of all time), Eudora Welty, and Anthony Burgess (best known for *A Clockwork Orange*, which remains as shocking today as it was in 1962, when it was first published). John Updike wrote that Green's novels made "more of a stylistic impact on me than those of any writer living or dead."

Henry Green died at age sixty-eight in 1973 and is largely forgotten. The books he influenced continue to be read and themselves inspire new works.

Sometimes books wear their influences loudly, mentioning other books by name, like *Pride and Prejudice and Zombies*. Sometimes the lineage is subtler, and the careful reader must tease out or guess at the influences. (How much of J. K. Rowling's Harry Potter series was inspired by the classic 1857 boarding-school novel *Tom Brown's School Days*, by Thomas Hughes?) And sometimes authors hint at influences that aren't really influences at all but instead speak to the kind of book the author would have *liked* to have written.

Whenever I read, I try to be aware of these echoes and associations and aspirations. How did this book come to be? What books does this book resemble, and what books does it bring to mind?

Then, as the reader, I become influenced while I'm reading. I'm not the same reader when I finish a book as I was when I started. Brains are tangles of pathways, and reading creates new ones. Every book changes your life. So I like to ask: How is this book changing mine?

At the trial in which he would be sentenced to death, Socrates (as quoted by Plato) said that the unexamined life isn't worth living. Reading is the best way I know to learn how to examine your life. By comparing what you've done to what others have done, and your thoughts and theories and feelings to those of others, you learn about yourself and the world around you. Perhaps that is why reading is one of the few things you do alone that can make you feel less alone; it's a solitary activity that connects you to others.

At fifty-four, I'm now roughly the same age Dante was when he was putting the finishing touches on *The Divine Com-*

edy. I'm the same age as von Aschenbach in Thomas Mann's *Death in Venice*. (I realized only recently that the character in this novella who was pining for a youth and his own lost youth was squarely in middle age; not having read the opening very carefully, I had always assumed that the "old" man who allowed the hotel barber to dye his hair jet black and garishly paint his face was in his seventies at the very least.) Fifty-plus is a good age for big questions. Unless I'm that rare soul who makes it past one hundred, I probably have less time ahead of me than I've already lived. Now that my brother, sister, and I are all over fifty, my brother, using a golf analogy, refers to our lives as being played on the back nine—the first nine holes are behind us. Whatever score we've accumulated, we carry with us. Suddenly, finishing honorably and staying out of the sand traps and water hazards matters more than seeing our names on the leaderboard.

On the other hand, I think any age is a good age for big questions. I asked some of my biggest and best when I was in high school and college—fittingly, as that's what school is for. I asked other big questions at painful times in my life— no age is immune from misfortune or feels it less keenly. And I hope and expect to be asking big questions right up to the end.

I know I'm not alone in my hunger for books to help me find the right questions to ask, and find answers to the ones that I have. Because I work in publishing and wrote a book about reading, I meet a lot of readers. Readers of all ages have shared with me their desire for a list of books to help guide them. I've heard from people who want classic novels to read; others just how-to books; others a list of titles from around the world. But most don't care what type of book or when it was written or by whom—they just want books that will help them find their way in the world and give them pleasure while they are at it.

On an endless and turbulent plane ride from New York to Las Vegas, I sat next to a nineteen-year-old West Point plebe. We started chatting, and he soon was telling me about some of his favorite books; *The Alchemist* by Paulo Coelho was one. I told him I also loved that fable of the shepherd who travels to Egypt in search of treasure. Our conversation quickly moved from pleasantries to the meaning of life. (Maybe *The Alchemist* prompted that; maybe it was because the turbulence was increasingly extreme.) As the plane bounced around the sky, I began to babble about other books that had inspired me. The cadet said he would trade me a genuine West Point baseball cap for a list of my favorite titles. I can't remember most of what I wrote down. I love the cap; I hope he liked the books.

And then there's my ninety-six-year-old friend Else, who is always ravenous for book recommendations. Recently, I told her about a book by Ruth Ozeki called *A Tale for the Time Being*. In this novel from 2013, a writer in the Pacific Northwest finds washed up on shore various items, including the diary of a sixteen-year-old girl in Tokyo who is being horribly bullied and is quite sure she doesn't want to go on living. The novel moves between the story of the writer, passages from the girl's diary, and a collection of letters that accompanied it. The most indelible character in the book is the girl's hundred-and-four-year-old grandmother, a quietly charismatic Zen Buddhist nun with a fascinating past, who provides physical and emotional sanctuary when life becomes too awful for the girl to bear alone.

Else also has enormous charisma, but of a more boisterous variety. (That is, she swears a lot.) And she too has lived a remarkable life: a teenage refugee from Nazi Germany, she became a music editor for film. Else read *A Tale for the Time Being* with delight and had much to say about it. But more than anything she wanted to discuss the hundred-and-four-year-old Buddhist nun. Else hung on to her every word, and declared her one of the most astonishing characters she had ever encountered in fiction or nonfiction—or in real life, for that matter. "Now I know who I want to be when I grow up," she announced to me gleefully, laughing and clapping her hands together.

As for me, I'm on a search—and have been, I now realize, all my life—to find books to help me make sense of the world, to help me become a better person, to help me get my head around the big questions that I have and answer some of the small ones while I'm at it.

I know that the West Point cadet, Else, and millions of others are on this search, too, a search that began long before I was born and that will continue long after I'm gone.

I'm not a particularly disciplined or systematic seeker. I don't give a great deal of thought to the books I choose—I'll read anything that catches my eye. Most of the time when I choose what I'm going to read it has absolutely nothing to do with improving myself. Especially when I'm at my happiest, I'm unlikely to search for a book to make me happier. But it's often during these periods of nonseeking that I've stumbled across a book that has changed my life.

I believe that everything you need to know you can find in a book. People have always received life-guiding wisdom from certain types of nonfiction, often from "self-help" books starting with the progenitor of the category, Samuel Smiles's 1859 bestseller *Self-Help (with illustrations of Character and Conduct)*. But I have found that all sorts of books can carry this kind of wisdom; a random sentence in a thriller will give me unexpected insight. (If I hadn't read *Killing Floor*, the masterful 1997 novel that introduced the world to Jack Reacher, a former military cop turned vagrant, I never would have learned this valuable piece of wisdom, which still guides me in work and life: "Waiting is a skill like anything else.")

I also believe that there is no book so bad that you can't find anything in it of interest. That, actually, is a paraphrase from the Roman lawyer Pliny the Younger, a sentiment later adopted by Miguel de Cervantes in *Don Quixote*. Admittedly, neither Pliny nor Cervantes were subject to some of the weakest "sex and shopping" books from the 1980s, but I still think it mostly holds true. You can learn something from the very worst books—even if it is just how crass and base, or boring and petty, or cruel and intolerant, the human race can be. Or even if it's just one gleaming insight in a muddy river of words.

There is a proud tradition of extracting lines from poetry and songs and using them in this way. And for centuries, people have kept "commonplace books": journals filled with transcriptions of quotes and extracts. But not everyone is a fan of cherry-picking odd passages from random books and using them to direct your life. Some people argue that lines from novels and plays are dependent on the context that surrounds them—that it's unseemly and self-serving to grab the odd line here and there, especially if it comes in the voice of a character and may not have anything to do with what the writer thinks. I don't buy this. It ignores the way that your brain collects, refracts, sorts, and combines information. Our search for meaning isn't limited to thoughts that were created to be meaningful and packaged in verse or easily extractable chunks. We can find meaning in everything—and everything is fair game. Your brain is, in fact, the ultimate commonplace collection, and everything you've ever read is in there somewhere, ready to come back into your consciousness when you want or need it.

So I spend my life collecting books and sentences from them: books I've sought alongside ones I've stumbled across, and sentences I've forced into my brain through rote memorization alongside ones that just found their way in by themselves.

At home, I'm a librarian, forever curating my collection.

Outside of my apartment, I'm a bookseller—hand-selling my favorite books to everyone I encounter.

There's a name for someone who behaves the way I do: Reader.

This book you are now reading is a manifesto of sorts—my manifesto, a manifesto for readers. Because I think we need to read and to be readers now more than ever.

We overschedule our days and complain constantly about being too busy; we shop endlessly for stuff we don't need and then feel oppressed by the clutter that surrounds us; we rarely sleep well or enough; we compare our bodies to the artificial ones we see in magazines and our lives to the exaggerated ones we see on television; we watch cooking shows and then eat fast food; we worry ourselves sick and join gyms we don't visit; we keep up with hundreds of acquaintances but rarely see our best friends; we bombard ourselves with video clips and emails and instant messages; we even interrupt our interruptions.

When it comes time for us to decide what we should buy and how we should spend our free time, we expect ever more choice. And in order to try to make our way through all of the options we've created for ourselves, we've turned the whole world into an endless catalog of "picks and pans," in which anything that isn't deemed to be mind-blowing is regarded as useless. We no longer damn things with faint praise—we damn them with any praise that is less than ecstatic. Loving or loathing are the defaults—five stars or one.

And at the heart of it, for so many, is fear—fear that we

are missing out on something. Wherever we are, there's someone somewhere doing or seeing or eating or listening to something better.

I'm eager to escape from this way of living. And I think if enough of us escape this, the world will be better for it. Connectivity is one of the great blessings of the Internet era, and it makes extraordinary things possible. I have a world of information keystrokes away; I can buy and sell and trade and share online; and when I drive in a foreign place I have a knowledgeable voice to guide me and to "recalculate my route" when I've gone astray. It would be impossible to list all the ways our lives have been transformed.

But connectivity is one thing; *constant* connectivity is another. I alert others when I am going to go "off the grid" for a few days or even, sometimes, for a couple of hours; the implication is that unless you are notified otherwise, you can assume I am always on it. Constant connectivity can be a curse, encouraging the lesser angels of our nature. None of the nine Muses of classical times bore the names Impatience or Distraction.

Books are uniquely suited to helping us change our relationship to the rhythms and habits of daily life in this world of endless connectivity. We can't interrupt them; we can only interrupt ourselves while reading them. They are the expression of an individual or a group of individuals, not of a hive mind or collective consciousness. They speak to us, thoughtfully, one at a time. They demand our attention. And they demand that we briefly put aside our own beliefs and prejudices and listen to someone else's. You can rant against a book, scribble in the margin, or even chuck it out the window. Still, you won't change the words on the page.

The technology of a book is genius: the order of the words is fixed, whether on the page or on-screen, but the speed at which you read them is entirely up to you. Sure, this allows you to skip ahead and jump around. But it also allows you to slow down, savor, and ponder.

We all ask each other a lot of questions: "Where did you go for vacation?" "How did you sleep?" Or, my favorite, as I eye the last bites of chocolate cake on a friend's dessert plate, "Are you going to finish that?" (A question memorably featured in the 1982 movie *Diner*.) But there's one question I think we should ask of one another a lot more often, and that's "What are you reading?"

It's a simple question but a powerful one, and it can change lives, creating a shared universe for people who are otherwise separated by culture and age and by time and space.

I remember a woman who told me that she was delighted to be a grandmother but was feeling sadly out of touch with her grandson. She lived in Florida. He and his parents lived elsewhere. She would call him and ask him about school or about his day. He would respond in one-word answers: Fine. Nothing. Nope.

And then one day she asked him what he was reading. And

he had just started *The Hunger Games*, a series of dystopian young adult novels by Suzanne Collins. The grandmother I met decided to read the first volume, so she could talk about it with her grandson the next time they chatted on the phone. She didn't know what to expect, but found herself hooked from the first pages when Katniss Everdeen volunteers to take her younger sister's place in the annual battle-to-the-death among a select group of teens.

The book helped this grandmother cut through the superficialities of phone chat and engage her grandson on the most important questions humans face about survival and destruction and loyalty and betrayal and good and evil, and about politics as well. And it helped her grandson engage with his grandmother on these same issues—not as a child in need of a lecture, but as a fellow seeker. It gave him a language for discussing issues that he was pondering, without having to explain exactly why these themes spoke to him.

When they talked about *The Hunger Games*, they were no longer just grandmother and grandson: they were two readers embarked on a journey together. Now her grandson couldn't wait to talk to her when she called—to tell her where he was, to find out where she was, and to speculate about what would happen next.

The Hunger Games gave them inspiration for deeper discussions than they had ever had, and it provided them a wealth of prompts for their conversations. The book even led them to talk about topics that included economic inequality, war, privacy, and the media. As they continued reading and talking about other books, they discovered they had an ever-expanding common language: their "vocabulary" was made up of all the characters and actions and descriptions in all the books they'd read, and they could employ these to convey their thoughts and feelings.

Other than the accident of family, they had never had much in common. Now they did. The conduit was reading.

When we ask one another "What are you reading?" sometimes we discover the ways that we are similar; sometimes the ways that we are different. Sometimes we discover things we never knew we shared; other times we open ourselves up to exploring new worlds and ideas. "What are you reading?" isn't a simple question when asked with genuine curiosity; it's really a way of asking, "Who are you now and who are you becoming?"

What follows are stories of books I've discovered that have helped me and others in ways big and small with some of the specific challenges of living in our modern world, with all its noise and distractions. Some are undoubtedly among the great works of our time. Others almost certainly are not. Many of the books I write about are books I first read when I was young. I'm not just a fifty-something-year-old reader; I'm the reader I was at every age I've ever been, with all the books I've ever read and all the experiences I've ever had constantly shifting and recombining in my brain. Often I remember exactly where I was when I first read a book that became important to me and also recall concurrent events, significant or not; other times I remember nothing else but how that book made me feel, and those same feelings come back whenever I think of that title.

Just as a Freudian psychiatrist might look to your childhood to help you interpret your desires and motivations, so I feel we need to look to the books we read as children to help us understand why we read the way we do. But it's not just childhood books that loom especially large in my life. Sometimes the last book I've read is the most important book I've ever read—but only until the *next* very important book I read. What is fresh initially can seem more profound; over time, though, my brain will discount newness in favor of resonance.

Some of these are not works I would list among my favorite books, but they are all books that I found (or that found me) when I needed them, or that prompted me to remember something, realize something, or see my life and the world differently. Every reader can construct a list like this; and that list may change from year to year or even week to week. Compiling and constantly revising this kind of book list is an exercise I highly recommend: it's a path to creating your own practical philosophy.

Some people have one book that they turn to again and again, one book that has all the answers. Most commonly, it is a book central to a particular faith: perhaps the Bible, the Bhagavad Gita, the Koran, or the like. I'm skeptical about finding any one book that will give me the answer to every question I have. Instead, I'm more likely to look to all sorts of different books to help me answer a multitude of questions. I doubt I will ever find a single book that's the literary equivalent of a Ginsu knife (that piece of cutlery catapulted to fame by an infomercial in my youth: it slices, it dices, it cuts cans and wood, and it never loses its edge). Both when cooking and reading, I enjoy a wide array of special tools and implements—whether I use them as intended or not. (A melon baller lends itself to all sorts of uses in addition to balling melons: making butter curls; apportioning cookie dough; separating artichoke flesh from choke.)

There's a particular kind of hope I sometimes have when I start a book. It's that maybe, just maybe—even though it goes against all my experience to date—I might be starting the one book that gives me all the answers I'll ever need. It could happen. My Ginsu knife. My Holy Grail.

Perhaps it might even be the book I frantically grab, unsure if I'll be interested or not, in the few seconds I have at an airport bookstore as I'm racing to the gate to board a flight.

I do believe that my Holy Grail of books could be out there—and I intend to keep reading until I find it. Of course, I'll keep reading after I do, too, because—well, because I love to read. I also believe that the Holy Grail of books won't be the greatest book ever written—I am certain there isn't such a thing. I think it will simply be a book that speaks perfectly to me at the moment I most need it and continues to speak to me for the rest of my life.

No book has ever done that for me, but one has come

close: *The Importance of Living* by a scholar named Lin Yutang, a book about Chinese culture and the "noble art of leaving things undone."

There is no book I turn to more often, which is why I begin this book with it and return to it again and again.

The Importance of Living
Slowing Down

EVERY NOW AND THEN the universe tells you what book you need to read; it does this by placing the name of that book and author in front of you in various contexts, until you can't help but take note. You ignore book recommendations from the universe at your peril. So after a decade of sporadically encountering the name Lin Yutang but still knowing almost nothing about him, I decided to investigate.

Starting in my teens, I had become obsessed with the writers of the 1930s, prompted initially by my fascination with the 1972 movie *Cabaret* and its boyishly handsome star, Michael York. *Cabaret* was based on two short novels by Christopher Isherwood, thinly fictionalizing his life in pre-Nazi Berlin. I read everything I could by Isherwood and about Berlin and about that decade and its writers; and the more I read, the more I came across the name Lin Yutang, alongside mentions of his second book, *The Importance of Living*.

Finally, when I was in my twenties, off to the library I

went to learn more about Lin Yutang. This was all, of course, pre-Internet.

I found out that *The Importance of Living* had been published by John Day publishers in 1937. Lin had become a friend of author Pearl Buck in Shanghai—and she had helped arrange for his books to be published. Buck was by then one of the world's bestselling authors. Her novel *The Good Earth*, set in a Chinese village, had won the Pulitzer Prize in 1932, and she would go on to win the Nobel Prize in Literature in 1938. She was also married to the founder of John Day publishers. Pearl Buck introduced Lin to her husband, who promptly offered him a contract.

By the time I went to investigate, *The Importance of Living* had been out of print for decades. But my local library had a well-worn copy ready for loan. It took some time to adjust to the chattiness of the book and its meandering digressions. When I first began to read it, it seemed charming but dated, a bit precious, verbose, contrarian for the sake of being contrarian, scattered, and peculiar. But soon I realized that beneath the chatter was profound wisdom and a radical rejection of the philosophy of ambition, which is so much a part of our culture.

The Importance of Living is a book that makes a case for loafing, for savoring food and drink, for not striving too much. Lin wanted an antidote to the raw competitiveness and frenetic activity he saw all around him in the early 1930s—not just in China, where he had grown up, but also in France and Germany, where he had worked and studied, and in the United States, where he had briefly attended college as a young man and where he was living when he wrote this book. Lin was eager to give people a framework for enjoying life, and he built it using the wisdom of ancient Chinese literature as well as a large helping of common sense.

Lin's book quickly became a success of epic proportions in the 1930s—one of those books read seemingly by everyone all over the world, translated into multiple languages, and one of the biggest bestsellers of its time.

Lin described his book as "a personal testimony, a testimony of my own experience of thought and life." He proudly proclaimed that he was not original and that the ideas he expressed "have been thought and expressed by many thinkers of the East and West over and over again." As for his methods, he wrote, "It is my habit to buy cheap editions of old, obscure books and see what I can discover there. If the professors of literature knew the sources of my ideas, they would be astounded at the Philistine. But there is a greater pleasure in picking up a small pearl in an ash-can than in looking at a large one in a jeweler's window." It's a manifesto, but also a commonplace book, of sorts.

He made clear that he was not a philosopher nor well read in philosophy and that, "technically speaking," his method and training were totally wrong. As for the sources for his philosophy? He credits his "cook's wife; a lion cub in the zoo; a squirrel in Central Park in New York; a deck steward who made one good remark," among several others.

Lin claimed to present "the Chinese point of view," which

he described as "an idle philosophy born of an idle life, evolved in a different age." This is the wisdom of a thousand years of scholar-poet-artists. And while he made no claim for its applicability outside of China, he wrote that he is "quite sure that amidst the hustle and bustle of American life, there is a great deal of wistfulness, of the divine desire to lie on a plot of grass under tall beautiful trees of an idle afternoon and *just do nothing*." The quote from Lin that at first seems to sum up his philosophy is this: "If you can spend a perfectly useless afternoon in a perfectly useless manner, you have learned how to live."

This book is encyclopedic. Lin has opinions on how to dress (he favors the loose, comfortable light robes of the Chinese scholar that don't cinch you at your stomach, the way Western pants with their tight belts do, particularly for men); how to decorate your home; what drinking games are best. His detours cover celibacy (which he proclaims unnatural) and include an apology, of sorts, for cannibalism. ("The difference between cannibals and civilized men seems to be that cannibals kill their enemies and eat them, while civilized men kill their foes and bury them, put a cross over their bodies and offer up prayers for their souls.")

Lin sought to inspire the reader toward idleness, contemplation, enjoyment of friends and tea and wine, reading, and nature. But he's quite exacting and specific. You can't just do these things—you have to do them with the correct form and spirit. One of the most persuasive chapters in the book is in the section called "The Enjoyment of Living," and that is an essay on lying in bed.

"Now what is the significance of lying in bed, physically and spiritually? Physically, it means a retreat to oneself, shut up from the outside world, when one assumes the posture most conducive to rest and peace and contemplation. There is a certain proper and luxurious way of lying in bed. Confucius, that great artist of life, [said that he] 'never lay straight' in bed 'like a corpse,' but always curled up on one side."

Lin continues:

> I believe one of the greatest pleasures of life is to curl up one's legs in bed. The posture of the arms is also very important, in order to reach the greatest degree of aesthetic pleasure and mental power. I believe the best posture is not lying flat on the bed, but being upholstered with big soft pillows at an angle of thirty degrees with either one arm or both arms placed behind the back of one's head. In this posture any poet can write immortal poetry, any philosopher can revolutionize human thought, and any scientist can make epoch-making discoveries.
>
> It is amazing how few people are aware of the value of solitude and contemplation. The art of lying in bed means more than physical rest for you, after you have gone through a strenuous day, and complete relaxation, after all the people you have met and interviewed, all the friends who have tried to crack silly jokes, and all your brothers and sisters who have tried to rectify your behavior and sponsor you

into heaven have thoroughly got on your nerves. It is all that, I admit. But it is something more. If properly culti-vated, it should mean a mental house-cleaning.

Rather than rushing off for work every morning, believed Lin, those in business should spend an extra hour in bed, thinking, planning, reviewing, so that when they arrive at work they are masters of their own destiny and not slaves to their schedules. For thinkers and inventors, he believed this morning lounging to be even more important. "A writer could get more ideas for his articles or his novel in this pos-ture than he could by sitting doggedly before his desk morn-ing and afternoon."

Far beyond the benefit of increased productivity, Lin also believed that lying in bed provided the best chance to listen to music, the birds, and the sounds of the village or city all around that may float in through your window.

Despite (or, trusting Lin as I do, *because of*) all this loaf-ing, Lin led a wildly productive and singular life, producing a prodigious amount of work throughout his many years (arti-cles, essays, books, and even novels) while shuttling back and forth between continents and religions. This in itself intrigued me—because I've always felt that people who have moved from one country to another, either as immigrants or refugees, have perspectives that others lack; and that people who have explored several faiths, not just the one they inher-ited, may have thought more deeply about faith than the rest of us. Lin was a seeker in politics, too, never aligned with any party for very long: he was always on the lookout for corruption (which he almost always found).

Lin Yutang was born in China in 1895, the fifth of eight children. His father had been illiterate as a young adult but taught himself to read and write, eventually becoming a Christian pastor with his own church in a remote part of Longxi County, Fujian Province. As a young boy, Lin would jump into his father's pulpit and deliver speeches to the congregation; from his earliest years, he was in love with language.

Lin studied Christian theology at a Western-style university in China but soon grew embittered, feeling that he had been denied exposure to the great Chinese culture from which he came. From then on, he studied Chinese literature and culture and followed the Tao and Buddhism. While he was in college, a beloved sister, who had been denied a college education by their father and thus had no choice but to marry, died of the plague while eight months pregnant. From then on, Lin became a crusader for higher-educational opportunities for women and also decided to devote himself to battling for social justice.

In 1919, Lin went to Harvard, but only for a time, dropping out because he couldn't afford the tuition and then moving to Paris to work. Soon, he found his way back to school and received his M.A. and Ph.D. in Germany, writing his thesis in German on the subject of Chinese philology. But he then returned to China, in 1923, to teach, interrupted by a short stint with the Nationalist government. He continued teaching in Shanghai and also began to write frequently for a magazine he founded, contributing many columns in Chinese critical of the Nationalist government. It was in Shanghai, in 1933, that he met Pearl Buck, who was a fan of his columns. In 1935, following the success of *My Country and My People*, his first book (the *New York Times* would later write that it "burst like a shell over the Western world"), Lin moved to New York and wrote a whole slew of books including *The Importance of Living* and one about Chinese Americans and another, published in 1943, called *Between Tears and Laughter* that was critical of America for its racist policies at home and around the world.

During World War II, Lin traveled to China and reported from there, now praising the Nationalists. But he was obsessed at that time by the desire to create a Chinese type-writer, something that had never been thought possible: Chinese is a language that requires thousands of individual characters in order to print a newspaper, as compared with twenty-six letters for English.

Lin sunk into that effort every cent he had made from all of his bestsellers but failed after repeated tries to create a prototype that could be manufactured for an affordable price. Still, his concept and mechanics were used for code-breaking and transcription machines. Thanks to his investment in the machine, he and his wife found themselves bankrupt after the war with three daughters to support in New York City. Financial salvation came in 1948 when he was offered a job as head of UNESCO's Arts and Letters Division in Paris. He loathed having to wake up in the morning and go to an office, but he had no choice.

In later life, Lin's finances would recover sufficiently to allow him to return to writing and scholarship. He would oversee the creation of the first major modern Chinese-English dictionary, a mammoth task. And he would for a time live in Singapore, running the new National University there.

In the 1950s, Lin came back to New York and converted back to Christianity. He continued to live in New York with his wife and three daughters. In 1966, he moved to Taipei, where he died, age eighty, in 1976.

His youngest daughter describes his final years in Taipei as among his happiest. General Chiang Kai-shek, the country's leader, had welcomed him warmly and even built a house for him according to Lin's own design; Madame Chiang was very fond of Lin Yutang and especially of Liao Tsuifeng, Lin's wife.

Chiang had also provided them with a chauffeur and maid (who also served as cook). The chauffeur and the maid fell in love, got married, and had a baby, whom Lin and Liao adored. Lin was still working on his massive Chinese dictionary at the time. As his daughter describes, "my father would knock off work in the afternoon, and my parents would then go for a walk. And the way they did it was ideal: The chauffeur would drive them to a lovely, wooded road, and my parents would then have their walk, and the chauffeur would follow in his car. They would walk for exactly as long as they found pleasant; then hop in the car and be driven home."

Today, almost no one I know of any age outside of China, Taiwan, and Hong Kong has read anything by Lin Yutang or even heard of him. When I queried one of my aunts about him, though, she instantly recalled that he had been the speaker at her high-school graduation, in New York, in 1936. She remembered just one piece of advice from his speech: he told the graduating class that, no matter what, they must travel—whether they felt they could afford to or not.

If Lin sensed the urgent need to slow down in the 1930s, it's clear he would feel it even more today. And not just in America, where Lin lived when he wrote *The Importance of Living*, but in every industrialized country of the world.

Right outside my apartment is a pocket park. It's a tiny triangle, with a sculpture of a World War I doughboy in the center. For decades, it was just a little patch of concrete, but more recently the neighbors came together and created a lovely little garden there: a lushly planted mound of green surrounded by park benches. In the spring there is a bright bristle of tulips; in the summer, exotic native grasses; in the fall, a jack-o'-lantern festival timed with Halloween; and in all three of those seasons, the park is shaded by elegant mature trees that turn in late fall the glorious colors trees turn. Just the kind of place to sit and do nothing.

And yet, almost no one who sits there is doing nothing. Few people look at the sculpture or any of the plantings; what they look at are their hands—or, rather, the phones cradled in their hands. They are texting, emailing, posting, pinning, tweeting, swiping.

And I must admit I am often one of them. We bring the hustle and bustle with us everywhere we go.

Sure, sometimes what I am texting about or photographing or pinning *are* the plants in front of me. I like to believe that when I pause and take a picture of one of the flowers in this pocket park, I'm seeing it differently, maybe appreciating it more, looking at it with the photographer's eye. That's true some of the time. But my thoughts swiftly leave the flower and go to where to send the photo or post it. While I'm doing that, I just sneak a look at others' postings, their parks and flowers and children. Oh, here's a snarky comment. I wonder what that's about? Soon I'm off, into the Internet, and out of my park—getting amused or aggravated in a way that I could be anywhere. I want what Lin thinks I want—to do nothing. Why should that be so hard?

As Lin confirms, it's always been hard. My behavior is nothing new. And I can't blame it solely on the devices.

Even when I leave my iPhone in my pocket, I still have trouble sitting and doing nothing. The hustle and bustle again comes with me, in my mind. What I am struck by again and again reading *The Importance of Living* is that it calls for a fundamental shift not in how I behave—when I look at my cell phone; when I don't—but in how I think about everything.

Take Lin's love of lying in bed. Lying in bed isn't an activity—it's a way of slowing down life. You can ponder, listen, or even read. So it's while lying in bed that I often read *The Importance of Living*. It's a book that lends itself to short-burst reading. Every few pages there's some sentence that keeps me thinking for hours, or intermittently throughout the day. For example, "I consider the education of our senses and our emotions rather more important than the education of our ideas."

The more I read *The Importance of Living*, the more I realize it's quite the opposite of an idle philosophy. It's a book that lives up to the promise of its title.

Stuart Little
Searching

THESE DAYS many of us do most of our searching with a keyboard. If we need to find something, the first thing we do is type some words into a box on a screen and hit ENTER. But that's really asking, not searching. The computer does the searching for us—offering either, increasingly, an actual answer (the movie starts at 7:00 p.m.) or a list of sites that might have your answer (the local cineplex). It's not the same as leaving the comfort of my home in search of something— something concrete or perhaps abstract—something I know is out there or only hope might be. The physical search involves an important set of tools that the computer search doesn't require: fortitude, patience, persistence, and commitment. In a word: character.

Whenever I think about searching, true searching, I think about Stuart Little.

At age five, I first encountered and fell in love with *Stuart Little*, E. B. White's novel about a mouse born to a New York family. That a human family should have a mouse as a child goes almost entirely without comment in the book. Stuart is simply the newest member of the Little family, albeit a rather small one. Accommodations—including "a tiny bed [built] out of four clothespins and a cigarette box"—are made as a matter of course.

When it's time to weigh Stuart, Mrs. Little uses a scale originally intended for weighing letters. "At birth Stuart could have been sent by first class mail for three cents, but his parents preferred to keep him rather than send him away." Fearing that Stuart isn't gaining weight fast enough, his mother takes him to a doctor who is delighted to meet him, merely remarking that it is "very unusual for an American family to have a mouse." And that's really all anyone has to say on the matter; Stuart may be small, he may be a mouse, but he's the Littles' child, and that's that.

This expression of unconditional love is, I suspect, one of the things that drew me to the book. I think I may have sensed even back then that at its heart *Stuart Little* is a tale of radical acceptance—you can be whatever or whoever you are born to be and not risk losing your family. Every child is in some ways different from her or his parents—even if not so different as Stuart was from his.

Why I *suspect* this is one of the things that drew me to the book—as opposed to knowing it—is twofold. First, I don't remember most of what I thought and felt at five. And second, this thought occurred to me really only after reading a groundbreaking book by Andrew Solomon called *Far from the Tree*, in which Solomon explores the difference between what he calls vertical identities (those you share with your parents) and horizontal identities (the ones you share with others but *not* with your parents). Stuart's vertical identity included being a member of the Little family and growing up in a pleasant part of New York City. His horizontal identities included being, well, a rodent—an attribute his parents and brother didn't share. To know that whatever your horizontal identities might be they can be accepted by your family is a comforting thought, whether conscious or not.

But I'm sure that what drew me most to this book was Stuart himself, one of the great characters in children's or any literature. He's brave, dapper, stoic, soft-spoken, well mannered, charming, adventuresome, matter-of-fact, and, above all, loyal. Whether locked in a refrigerator, rolled up in a curtain, piloting a model boat on a stormy pond in Central Park and freeing it after a dreadful collision, or motoring off in a small car, searching the country for his beloved friend and onetime savior, the bird Margalo, Stuart experiences strong emotions but only once loses his cool. And that is the time he is facing almost certain death.

At first, Stuart takes his impending end in relative stride. When he realizes that he has, through bad luck and timing, been dumped onto a trash scow that is being towed out to sea, he thinks, "Well . . . this is about the worst thing that could happen to anybody." He realizes he's going to die and would rather not do it covered in banana peels and other trash. But that's all bearable. It's only when he realizes he will never see his family and friends again, never experience again the comforts of home, that he becomes inconsolable and starts sobbing. And that's when Margalo swoops in to the rescue.

Quickly, Stuart is back to his practical self. As Margalo prepares to fly him off the barge, he has a few questions:

"Suppose I get dizzy," said Stuart.

"Don't look down," replied Margalo. "Then you won't get dizzy."

"Suppose I get sick at my stomach."

"You'll just have to *be* sick," the bird replied. "Anything is better than death."

"Yes, that's true," Stuart agreed.

The next time Stuart feels an intense emotion, it is heartbreak; Margalo, in peril, leaves without being able to say goodbye, and Stuart doesn't know where she's gone or why—but knows he must find her. Stuart is so stricken that he can't eat or sleep. He resolves to do whatever he has to do to find the friend who saved his life, even if that means leaving his family and the comforts of home behind. Here's where his practical self reemerges—while he's searching for Margalo he might as well try to seek his fortune at the same time.

Most of the characters I had hitherto encountered in children's fiction had been representative of one and only one character trait—they were brave *or* funny, confident *or* curious, adventuresome *or* retiring. In contrast, like the best and truest characters in life and fiction, Stuart contains multitudes. But one of his most prominent characteristics is kindness. If Stuart became the ruler of the world, he proclaims, he would make a law that everyone has to be kind (even knowing that most people wouldn't follow it). That doesn't mean he isn't prepared to spring with bow and arrow to the defense of a friend—but he behaves cordially throughout until he has good reason to act otherwise.

While Stuart's gallantry remains constant, other aspects of his personality change. At the start, he's very much the family man. But he takes to life on the road and comes to see himself as a free soul; you might even call him a hobo.

As Stuart explains to a storekeeper he meets in a small town, "I'm not much of a society man these days. Too much on the move. I never stay long anywhere—I blow into a town and blow right out again, here today, gone tomorrow, a will o' the wisp. The highways and the byways are where you'll find me, always looking for Margalo."

For those few unlucky readers who didn't get to meet Stuart when they were young, and haven't yet, you won't want to read my next sentence or the rest of this chapter. At the end of the book, you discover that Stuart's search is inconclusive, but what's important is that he is still searching. Ultimately, Stuart is a romantic, a mouse with a cause, a seeker, alone, on the road, heading north—because that, he learns, is the way you head when you don't know exactly where you are going.

I remember loving books before I read *Stuart Little* (or,

rather, had it read to me). But I don't remember ever so completely wanting to emulate a character in a book before encountering Stuart. He was my first fictional role model.

Less happily, Stuart also gave me my first lesson in the many ways real life doesn't always follow the scripts of the books we read and can be deeply disappointing by comparison.

My obsession with E. B. White's book at age five led me to believe that all I needed for complete happiness was a Stuart Little of my own, so I first asked and then begged my parents to find one for me. At the time, the popular rodent pet was a gerbil.

I promised my parents that I would take excellent care of my gerbil. How could I not? He would be my best friend. I would clean his cage religiously. I would give him water and feed him. We would be best pals. I wouldn't ever ask for anything again. At night, I even prayed for this gerbil. If I was truly good, then God would give me a gerbil. And not just any gerbil: a dapper, brave, funny, adventuresome, and kind gerbil.

Finally, for my birthday, my parents bought me a gerbil. He was adorable. Everything I ever could have wanted. At first.

One evening, a few days after the gerbil's arrival, I reached into his cage to hold him. I guess he didn't want to be held right then, because he bit my finger. Hard. And there was blood.

I quickly withdrew my hand. I closed the cage door. He looked at me. I looked at him. And then I burst into tears.

The assault had taken place at cocktail hour, and I suspect the adults found the whole event somewhat charming. After my injured finger was Band-Aided, they went back to drinking, and I went back to my room. My gerbil looked at me. I looked at him. And I grew unhappier and unhappier with the present state of affairs.

Partly it was the gerbil's disloyalty. He had betrayed me! Partly it was shame. Why was no one else surprised that this had happened? And partly it was the indifference of the adult world to my pain and suffering. I had been mauled, and no one seemed to care.

There seemed to be only one solution: I had to leave home, leave my gerbil, and leave the misery behind me. I went to the closet, climbed up on a chair, found my suitcase, threw some clothes into it, zippered it shut, and headed out the door, dragging it behind me. Where I was going, I would figure out later. But it was time to go.

At that time, we lived in a house in Cambridge, Massachusetts. Out I went, into the hot summer evening. Then, at about fifty yards, I paused. There was the house, my house. There was laughter from inside. The adults were still drinking. No one had even realized I had gone. I had thought I would leave my misery behind, but I was still miserable. And where was I going? All my life was in that house, even if its other inhabitants didn't always understand exactly how I was feeling.

My parents later claimed that they saw me leave and kept an eye on me out the window, figuring that it was better for me to come back by myself than to be coaxed back. They were always a little fuzzy on the details after that, but clearly I came home. Soon, it was one of those funny family stories—the time that Will got bit by his gerbil, packed his case, and ran away. Oh, and the gerbil lived—as long as gerbils generally live. I fed him; cleaned his cage; gave him water. But we never really bonded. I'm not sure gerbils ever really bond with humans.

Fortunately, this misadventure didn't diminish my love for Stuart Little one bit. Stuart was a mouse, after all— a mouse who could sail a boat and drive a roadster—not a gerbil. And a fictional character. And even if not, I could hardly hold the entire rodent group responsible for the viciousness of one gerbil. So I had learned nothing about Stuart from my unfortunate experience. But I did have occasion later to think more about our respective decisions to leave home. When Stuart left, he was on a quest. When I left, I was running away. And when you are running away from something, it often ends up coming with you, especially if the thing you are running away from is your own behavior.

Stuart Little was E. B. White's first book for children. Prior to writing it, he was working for *The New Yorker* and *Harper's Magazine* and was one of the most admired essayists in America. (He would later cowrite with William Strunk Jr. what is widely regarded as the best style guide for writers: *The Elements of Style*. He would also later write two more classic books for children: *Charlotte's Web* and *The Trumpet of the Swan*.)

In a letter to Anne Carroll Moore, the then current and

first children's librarian ever at the New York Public Library, White wrote in February 1939 that he had been at work for years on a book for children—but only when he was ill. He confessed that he had great fear about writing for children, as "one can so easily slip into a cheap sort of whimsy or cuteness. I don't trust myself in this treacherous field unless I am running a degree of fever."

Two weeks later, in a letter accompanying an early draft he sent to his editor, he wrote, "It would seem to be for children, but I'm not fussy who reads it."

He would finally finish *Stuart Little* in 1943, and it would be published in 1945. But, as recounted in *Letters of E. B. White*, Moore, who had encouraged White, was terribly disappointed in the book when she read an advance copy of it—so much so that she told the book's editor that it "mustn't be published" and wrote to Katharine White, E.B.'s wife, urging her to convince her husband to stop the publication.

But she didn't and he didn't and the book would go on to sell more than four million copies in English alone.

About the inconclusive ending, E. B. White would later write to a teacher that it had "plagued" him, "not because I think there is anything wrong with it but because children seem to insist on having life neatly packaged. The final chapters were written many years after the early chapters and I think this did affect the narrative to some extent. I was sick and was under the impression that I had only a short time to live, and so I may have brought the story to a more abrupt close than I would have under different circumstances."

But White explained further: "My reason (if indeed I had

any) for leaving Stuart in the midst of his quest was to indicate that questing is more important than finding, and a journey is more important than the mere arrival at a destination. This is too large an idea for young children to grasp, but I threw it to them anyway. They'll catch up with it eventually. Margalo, I suppose, represents what we all search for, all our days, and never quite find."

White resisted all entreaties to write a sequel to *Stuart Little*. The hero's quest had to remain open-ended. I never craved a watertight ending, because I didn't much care whether Stuart found Margalo or not. What fascinated me wasn't Stuart's odyssey, but how he behaved while he was on it. The book ends with Stuart climbing into his car and heading north. White writes, "The sun was just coming up over the hills on his right. As he peered ahead into the great land that stretched before him, the way seemed long. But the sky was bright, and he somehow felt he was headed in the right direction."

This nonending is one of the most beautiful endings in all of literature.

Inspired by Stuart's quest, I've come up with some rules to live by. Most books don't lend themselves to this kind of treatment. But for me, *Stuart Little* does. Here they are:

Try not to run away but to go in search.

Try to remain polite when possible, as Stuart always does, and to accept what can't be changed—even though you might mourn what you're losing, the way Stuart did when he was on the garbage scow headed out to sea.

Try to dress smartly. (I usually fail miserably on that account: A friend once told me that I "wear my clothes well." English was his second language; he later clarified he'd meant that I wear them until they are worn out.)

Try to be as brave as Stuart, and as resourceful as he was when he piloted the model boat to victory.

But more than anything: Try to be as cheerful and optimistic as you can be in the face of whatever comes next.

The Girl on the Train
Trusting

I HAVE 2,391 "friends" on Facebook. People who don't enjoy social networking snort derisively at the idea of anyone maintaining a connection to 2,391 people; they think it's absurd that I would want to share snippets of my life with all these folk and would be interested to read about their likes and dislikes and their daily lives. With 2,391 Facebook friends, I couldn't be less far from the madding crowd; I invite it into my life every time I check my smartphone or turn on my computer. But I enjoy it—I get recommendations for recipes; I see pictures of homes and vacations and children; I give and get suggestions on what items to buy and where to eat; I marvel at the cuteness of the animal world as revealed in countless adorable posts. If it weren't for my Facebook friends, I never would have discovered the little Chinese girl who coos at animals in a hypnotic tone and, with voice and hand, can put into a sleeplike trance not just puppies and kittens but also chickens, rabbits, frogs, and lizards. It's also through

Facebook that I've learned about books that are now among my favorites and found links to articles that have changed and deepened my understanding of the world.

Obviously, most of the people sharing their clips and lives with me are not my friends in the traditional sense of the word. These are friendly acquaintances, and friends of friends. If they were really my friends, I could trust them all. Because that's my definition of a friend: someone I can trust.

Knowing whom to trust is not a new problem. But as more people gain access to our lives and attention through social networking, it's a problem that we need to ponder with increasing frequency. Those friendly acquaintances who want me to recommend them for a job or rent me an apartment for a night—can I rely on them to not embezzle from their new employer or to refrain from giving me bedbugs? Are their recommendations genuine, or are they flogging their wares for profit?

Trust is all about instinct. If you had all the facts, you wouldn't need trust. Trust is what is required in the absence of proof. But I believe you can strengthen your instincts by testing them; every time you prove yourself right or wrong, they grow stronger. I've discovered that a great way to test my instincts with regard to trustworthiness or lack thereof is by reading mystery novels and thrillers—like the 2015 novel *The Girl on the Train* by the British novelist Paula Hawkins.

Before I read *The Girl on the Train*, I already knew quite a lot about this novel. I knew that it was a thriller about a girl named Rachel who took "the same commuter train every morning and night." I knew that the train, every day, would stop at a signal that allowed her to view the same couple having breakfast on their deck and that she looked forward to this. And that she began to feel that she'd started to know them. I knew that she had names for them and had invented a scenario in which theirs was the perfect life.

I also knew that one day she would see something that would shock her. It would be for only a scant minute. Suddenly, everything would change. I knew that Rachel would go to the police. And I knew that soon she would be "deeply entangled not only in the investigation but in the lives of everyone involved." What I didn't know was whether by going to the police she'd done "more harm than good."

The reason I knew all of this is simple. That's what the publisher wanted me to know—this information is from the book flap on the American edition of the hardcover. Unless I had willfully decided not to read the flap, there's no way I could have *not* known this.

But I had heard about this novel even before I read the flap: it's rare to read any book without knowing *something* of it beforehand, whether from a friend, a review, a bookseller, or a comment online. And most people don't want to read a book unless they know a little something about it, even if only where it's set.

Once you begin reading *The Girl on the Train*, it soon becomes apparent that Rachel may be what people call an unreliable narrator. That is, she may or may not be telling the reader the truth. There's a great tradition of books featuring unreliable narrators: *The Good Soldier* by Ford Madox Ford, published in 1915, is the most influential; it's a brilliantly cynical novel about marriage and infidelity. Gillian Flynn's *Gone Girl*, a startling suspense novel from 2012, is another book that features an unreliable narrator, and also includes a deeply cynical view of marriage, with a considerably bloodier plot than *The Good Soldier*'s.

But if you've read *The Girl on the Train*, you know at the end whether Rachel has been honest or lying. If you haven't read it, I'm not going to tell you. You're going to have to read the book and try to figure it out as you go along. Rachel is jealous, often irrational, and obsessed with her ex; she is deeply flawed and deeply human, sympathetic and infuriating. You want to trust her, but she keeps giving you reasons not to. Just when you think you know what's going on, you realize maybe you don't.

That's why Rachel, like most unreliable narrators, is not really an unreliable narrator at all; she's a *possibly* unreliable narrator.

The fun of reading a book with a *possibly* unreliable narrator, as opposed to reading a book with a *certainly* unreliable narrator, is that you don't know for sure whether you are being told, in whole or in part, the truth. If you know for a fact that the narrator is unreliable, then that's not really an unreliable narrator at all; it's simply a dishonest one.

Rachel is one of three narrators in *The Girl on the Train*; what makes her particularly intriguing as the main character in a thriller is that she admits to lying in order to get people to take her story seriously ("If I admitted the truth, the trust would be gone") and that she is possibly lying even to herself. It's as though she's Sherlock Holmes and, maybe, the criminal Moriarty all in one. She drinks a lot of booze, and she frequently blacks out, and so she's not exactly sure what she has and hasn't witnessed or done.

At one point, she contemplates hypnosis. But she rejects that when her therapist tells her that memories "retrieved" (she tells us he puts air quotes around that word) through hypnosis can't always be trusted. She tells us, "I can't risk it. I couldn't bear to have other images in my head, yet more memories that I can't trust, memories that merge and morph and shift, fooling me into believing what is not, telling me to look one way when really I should be looking another way."

Perhaps her massive lack of clarity is among the reasons I (along with so many other readers) relate to Rachel. Most of us are sometimes uncertain about what we've done. In a world where we are bombarded with messages and constantly looking at screens, or a world in which we ourselves sometimes drink to excess, reality can blur, and sometimes we blur it. Did I read that? Did I send that text? Was that something I saw, read, or dreamed? Often we don't know. And that's frightening enough. What's even more frightening, though, is when we are sure of something that we saw, did, or read—and then find out that we couldn't have or didn't.

"I'm certain it was raining; we ate barbecue; and Jim told that funny story," I might say to my husband.

"Well, I'm certain that it was sunny; we ate burgers; and it was Mary who told that funny story," he might reply.

In a perfect world, we would both be wrong: the day would have been hazy; we would have eaten fried chicken; and Edgar would have told the tale. That would spare both of us the annoyance of hearing "I told you so" when the truth is revealed. More often, however, only one of us is remembering things inaccurately.

Finding out that you were wrong when you were sure you were right is like that moment in cartoons when a character runs off a cliff and freezes in midair for a few seconds before plummeting. There is a brief instant when you still hold on to the hope that you were right before conceding total wrongness—and it's only then that the ground falls out from under you.

If we can't always trust ourselves, then how can we ever trust anyone else?

The answer provided by thrillers is that, even when you are surrounded by strangers, eventually you may need to trust someone. And it's sometimes the last person you thought you could trust. In order to misdirect us, clever thriller writers give characters prejudices and biases that readers share. Ultimately, characters save themselves by breaking free of these. Maybe the government official isn't out to help you. Maybe the petty criminal on the corner is the only person who can save your life.

And so it goes with Facebook and all the people who enter our lives in person and on the Internet. Whom they know, what they do for a living, and how they look tell us very little about them. What they say about themselves tells us very little, too. Are they reliable or unreliable? Sometimes they don't even know themselves.

Novels like *The Girl on the Train* give us the tools we need to try to figure out whom we can trust, and whom to keep at electronic arm's length, helping us focus more on how our "friends" *behave* than on how they appear or what they say.

And here's one more thing I've learned from mysteries and thrillers: the only people you should never, ever trust are the people who say, "Trust me."

The Odyssey
Embracing Mediocrity

IN THE EARLY 1970S in the Boston area it wasn't unusual to start studying Latin in seventh grade. Almost all the schools, public and private, taught it. I suspect this had something to do with Boston's large and influential Irish Catholic population (even after the Second Vatican Council, which ended in 1965, Mass in Boston was still occasionally celebrated in Latin). Studying Latin was particularly not unusual at my school because we had the kind of Latin teacher who was so popular that he could have been teaching Uighur and his class still would have been filled to bursting with kids who wanted not just to take the class but to be able to say they had taken it, to trade stories with those who had sat in those seats before. So, at age twelve, I started Latin.

Literature is full of books about great teachers: *The Prime of Miss Jean Brodie* by Muriel Spark and *Goodbye, Mr. Chips* by James Hilton, to name just two. Mr. Gill, my seventh-grade Latin teacher, was the kind of inspired, charismatic teacher who deserves a book of his own.

"Ah, dawn breaks over Marblehead," Mr. Gill would say when you got an answer right. We thought this expression was a riot; Marblehead was a nearby Massachusetts town. We didn't just want to learn from Mr. Gill—we wanted to *be* him and would greet one another as he greeted us: "Hi, hi, how are you?" pronounced in his broad Boston accent as "Hi, hi, how ah yuh?" The answer was always: "Gud, gud, ya-self?"

Mr. Gill believed that students learn best when multiple senses are engaged, so he had us sing the Latin declensions in unison to allow us to hear them fully voiced; he also required each of us to create our own set of Latin-English flashcards so we could touch the words we were learning. Smell and taste were the senses he left out.

Each week after collecting our homemade flashcards, he would fling them back at us Frisbee-style, with uncanny aim. It was a point of pride not to fumble your set when it was tossed at you and also incentive to stay awake lest your cards go flying by while you were dozing.

We learned French to go to France (one day, we hoped). We learned history because, we were told, if we didn't we were destined to repeat it. We learned math so we could learn more math (at least that's how it was explained to us: if we didn't take geometry, we couldn't take trig, and if we didn't take trig, then we couldn't take calculus—no wonder I stopped as soon as I could, to my eternal regret). But Latin—Latin was going to teach us things. Exactly what? Well, that we had to wait to find out.

First came Caesar. From him I learned that Gaul was divided in three parts. And I learned a lot of military maneuvers and wondrous facts about the Roman Empire and neighboring nations. (According to Caesar, the barbarian men of early Britain dyed themselves a fierce shade of blue and shaved their entire bodies except for the hair on top of their head and their mustaches; they were also polygamous.) We spent a lot of time reading Caesar. It was very enjoyable. But Mr. Gill spoke with such reverence about what the classics had to teach us that I kept waiting for a piece of knowledge that would knock me off my chair. I was hoping that the thing I would learn would be something intense, that after a certain point I would become like a Mason, someone who had secrets and shares them with others who had been through the same rigorous initiation. And after I learned that thing, I hoped and trusted, my life would never be the same.

In the meantime, however, I started to glimpse a great truth: history was long and I was short. Caesar accomplished more than I ever possibly could; had written about it in timeless works; and would be read as long as people read. There was no chance I would possibly leave a mark on the world that measured up to Caesar's.

When I went to high school, at a boarding school, I decided to continue with Latin. And I decided to add ancient Greek. I had no good reason for this, just the belief that ancient Greek was truly hard core. If Latin was the Navy, ancient Greek was the Navy SEALs. And, besides, that meant that I would enter the orbit of another charismatic teacher: George Tracy.

Mr. Tracy was highly theatrical—he had been a Shake-spearean actor in Canada, the land of his birth. And he was notoriously tough. He didn't treat us as children; he treated us as adults who had simply neglected, as of yet, to learn all they were supposed to have learned. But when one of his students did show that she or he had learned something—well, then that student was bathed in light.

Traditionally, Greek is taught backward—or, rather, starting at the middle with Plato and moving back. Even though Homer came before Plato, schools would first teach you the kind of Greek Plato wrote and only later the Greek of Homer, more different from the Greek of Plato than Shakespeare's English is from ours.

Mr. Tracy taught differently. He started with Homer and then moved his students chronologically forward, through Plato, through the dramatists, and finally, in proper order, up to the (much easier) Greek of the New Testament.

This meant a few things. First, it meant that there was only one textbook available: *A Reading Course in Homeric Greek*. Every other book took the traditional approach of beginning with Plato. Written by Jesuits, this textbook had, as I recall, extremely odd practice sentences: "Had Jesus and Homer met, how well they would have gotten along!" (I remember taking a different view. I also remember wondering if Jesus might have cured Homer's blindness, whereupon Homer might have chosen a different profession altogether, and then we would never have had access to the great stories he left us.)

Second, it meant that we actually got to start our education with Homer: within months of beginning ancient Greek, I was translating bits of *The Iliad* into English. It was thrilling.

Granted, my translations were not ones for the ages.

> *What ho! Eternal Aegis-bearing Zeus's child,*
> *The Greeks spring forth towards their native land,*
> *To head for home o'er watery paths now wild,*
> *Leaving Helen to Priam and the Trojan's Hands.*

Where Mr. Gill might have gently suggested I go back to my vocabulary cards, Mr. Tracy scowled fiercely. He told me that there was no particular call for a modern translation of *The Iliad* that attempted to ape the style of Alexander Pope. I'm sure he added that modern English would do just fine and asked me to please, please stop rhyming and instead focus on the meaning of the words I was translating.

But I was hooked. If I was looking for the secret that would connect me to others around the world and across the ages, *The Iliad* and *The Odyssey* were it. Thrilling. This was a whole world I had no idea existed—a world of honor and hubris, lust and war, fidelity and betrayal. This was a deeply adult world, too, a world of violence, sex, and drugs.

First in my affections was Odysseus. Here was a real hero. He is wily, able to outsmart the Cyclops. He is strong, a leader of men. He perseveres. And he is deeply fallible, making a whole lot of flawed choices due to lust, pride, and bad judgment.

I was also quite taken with the idea of the land of the Lotus-eaters, where Odysseus stops and where he almost loses a portion of his crew. The land of the Lotus-eaters is a seeming paradise where time passes effortlessly; the visitor, happily drugged, forgets all thoughts of what he needs to do in life and abandons all plans to return home. Growing up in the shadow of the 1960s, I felt I understood the appeal of this land: I had met plenty of people just a few years older than I who had found themselves there and who hadn't been able to leave. Odysseus underscored the point that, though you can visit the land of the Lotus-eaters, the time *will* come when you definitely need to leave it. Of course, that's not always easy to do. But if you overstay that time, you may never be able to leave. Ever.

As Mr. Tracy guided us through *The Odyssey*, he had us keep one word foremost in our minds: "nostalgia." This was not the kind of nostalgia we speak of today, where you squeal with delight and only the slightest pang of longing when a song you slow-danced to in the 1970s—"Blame It on the Sun" by Stevie Wonder, perhaps, or "Landslide" by Fleetwood Mac—comes on the radio. Actually, even radios are cause for nostalgia today. No, this was nostalgia in the true meaning of the word: home pain. A longing that is so intense you experience it as you would the most severe malady. The child who sobs inconsolably on a night spent with strangers far from home, not knowing if she will ever return to the place where she grew up and the people who raised her, experiences the nostalgia of Odysseus. It's a homesickness that is so profound it causes almost unbearable pain.

How long can you stay in the land of the Lotus-eaters? How do you handle the pain when you don't know if you can ever get home or when your home is gone? I was starting to realize that reading Greek and Latin wasn't going to give me any single piece of knowledge that would astound me or one secret that would change my life; it was giving me instead something more valuable: a lifetime of questions.

Over the next few years, I continued to study classics: with Mr. Tracy; with an impassioned and engaging young colleague of his whom we called Doc Marshall (as though he were a character in a Western and not a Ph.D. in classics); and then with a series of eccentric professors all the way through college (one of whom was forbidden by his doctor from reading Thucydides because it made his heart race). But as much as I learned from the books I read and from these teachers over so many years, and as many great questions as I added to my repertoire, one of the most important things I learned came in my first few weeks with Mr. Tracy. And it was a lesson in learning.

The assignment was simple—a paper on some classical topic about which little is known or can be learned. But I'd worked hard (or, at least, many hours) on it and was convinced I had created a work of brilliance. As a result, I was excited to get the graded paper back a few days later—and then bitterly disappointed to discover that Mr. Tracy had given me a C.

I asked to see Mr. Tracy after class.

"Excuse me, sir," I said, somewhat tentatively. "But I really think I deserved a B."

Mr. Tracy looked at me with no discernible emotion; then he pulled out a big red felt-tip marker. He carefully crossed out the C. And then he wrote a big B and gave it back to me, but not before he paused and asked a key question: "Are you sure you don't want an A?"

Since I had not been prepared for a quick victory, and had a whole speech at the ready, I didn't know what to say. But then I realized where this was going.

Mr. Tracy waited a moment and then said, "It's a C paper. No matter what grade I put on it, it's still a C paper. But I'm happy to give it a B or even an A. In fact, why don't you just tell me what grade you want when you hand in each paper for the rest of the term and save me the trouble of grading them."

Then Mr. Tracy really went for it. "In fact, why don't you just tell me what grade you want for the whole course so you don't have to show up at all."

I had to beg Mr. Tracy to give me my C back. Eventually I got it.

What I thought I learned that afternoon was not to grade grub.

But on reflection, I now realize that what Mr. Tracy taught me that day was to recognize my mediocrity. And that, in fact, the essence of learning is to do just that.

A C means you've done average work. There's nothing shameful about being average. You didn't fail. You didn't even come close. You did what you were supposed to do. Cheerfully accepting the C means that you recognize there's such a thing as a B and an A and that you know you fell short of both; you can take pride in your place in the middle of the pack but still appreciate that there's room to grow.

Mediocrity isn't crass or shoddy or vulgar. It's, well, mediocre. There's nothing wrong with it. It's not bad. When you embrace mediocrity, you embrace humility—you learn to see that no matter how good you are at something, the world probably has people who are more talented at it than you. You can strive to learn from people who do things better, or you can at least appreciate them—even if you don't want to be them. By definition, most of us are mediocre, and everyone is mediocre at something.

It's often just a matter of perspective. The best pitcher on your local Little League team wouldn't last long on the mound in the major leagues. Great teachers help us see ourselves in the broadest perspective possible. Mr. Tracy may have wanted to teach me a lesson about my own arrogance, but he certainly wasn't trying to discourage me: He was trying to get me to see things as they really are. Encouragement comes in many forms, but excessive or unwarranted praise isn't encouragement.

The British essayist G. K. Chesterton, in his 1910 treatise *What's Wrong with the World*, wrote, "If a thing is worth doing, it is worth doing badly." Sure, it may be worth more done well, but if a thing is worth doing, it's worth doing no matter how well or badly you do it. It's just plain worth doing. When we denigrate mediocrity, we discourage ourselves and others from trying new things. It would be great to be a great painter, but it's also great just to paint. Or sing or throw pots or knit scarves or play chess.

That doesn't mean, though, we should lower our standards. In fact, it's partly this unwarranted horror of mediocrity that causes us to call things great that are merely good or fine. There are plenty of good slices of pizza to be had in Greenwich Village that are neither the best nor the worst slices in New York City. We don't have to pretend they are something more than tasty and filling to enjoy them. We might even want to try to make our own mediocre pizza from time to time.

And as for Odysseus, even he would have to admit that he didn't do a great job of getting home. Sure, he was a clever fellow but an arrogant one, too, a boaster and troublemaker. Others managed to come right home after the war chronicled in *The Iliad;* it took Odysseus ten years. He was held captive; he dawdled; he got lost. He was caught in storms. And he almost gave up his quest—to live with Circe, an enchantress who also happened to be an excellent cook.

But he does eventually make it back (with help from some gods) to Ithaca, where life is in massive disarray. The return is a solid C-level performance—far from an A, sure, but by no means a failure.

What I Talk About When I Talk About Running Napping

THE JAPANESE NOVELIST Haruki Murakami's intensely engrossing novels and stories are almost always dreamlike and often include fantastical ingredients: a man possessed by sheep, a glowing unicorn skull, alternate universes. They also often feature characters who have dropped out of society for one reason or another. After the international success of his third novel, *A Wild Sheep Chase*, which was published in 1982 when he was thirty-three years old, Murakami went on to publish ten more novels to date, all international best-sellers, including *The Wind-Up Bird Chronicle* and *Kafka on the Shore* and *1Q84*. Murakami has won just about every literary prize you can win short of the Nobel Prize for Literature, for which he is most bookies' favorite. He also writes short stories; translates other writers' books from English into Japanese; travels often; collects vinyl records; and sometimes teaches.

Murakami is a runner. He runs every day. And he runs marathons. In the introduction to his memoir of running and writing, *What I Talk About When I Talk About Running*, Murakami writes that running is "both exercise and a metaphor. Running day after day, piling up the races, bit by bit I raise the bar, and by clearing each level I elevate myself. At least that's why I've put in the effort day after day: to raise my own level. I'm no great runner, by any means. I'm at an ordinary—or perhaps more like mediocre—level. But that's not the point. The point is whether or not I improved over yesterday. In long-distance running the only opponent you have to beat is yourself, the way you used to be."

And Murakami is also a napper. As he writes later in this book, "One other way I keep healthy is by taking a nap. I really nap a lot. Usually I get sleepy right after lunch, plop down on the sofa, and doze off. Thirty minutes later I come wide-awake. As soon as I wake up, my body isn't sluggish and my mind is totally clear. This is what they call in southern Europe a siesta. I think I learned this custom when I lived in Italy, but maybe I'm misremembering, since I've always loved taking naps."

It's an anomalous passage in a book filled with descriptions of feats of physical strength and endurance. Murakami (translated by Philip Gabriel) chronicles a lifetime of running and writing, leading up to the New York marathon of 2006. It's a very personal work—not a self-help book as such, but one in which Murakami lets us see inside his head as he trains for marathons and runs in them, and as he writes.

He shares the music he listens to when he's running (occasionally jazz, but more often rock, including Red Hot Chili Peppers, Beck, the Beach Boys, and the Rolling Stones), his weight, what he drinks and eats (Sam Adams and Dunkin' Donuts while living and running in Boston), and the running shoes he wears (Mizuno).

More deeply, Murakami tackles the need for solitude, but also its corrosive dangers. He writes about anger, and how he handles it (he runs a little longer). He tells us something of his life, and the moment he chose to become a novelist—at a baseball game at 1:30 p.m. on April 1, 1978, right after a young American player named Dave Hilton hit a double. He writes, "And it was at that exact moment that a thought struck me: *You know what? I could try writing a novel.* I can still remember the wide open sky, the feel of the new grass, the satisfying crack of the bat. Something flew down from the sky at that instant, and whatever it was, I accepted it."

That was when Murakami was twenty-nine. He didn't start running until he was thirty-three: "The age that Jesus Christ died. The age that Scott Fitzgerald started to go downhill. That age may be a kind of crossroads in life."

In a particularly vivid section early in the book, Murakami recounts running between Athens and Marathon, the original marathon, the twenty-six-mile route a Greek messenger is said to have run in 490 BCE to let the government in Athens know about the victory over the Persians in the Battle of Marathon. Murakami runs it in reverse, ending where the messenger began. It's the first time he's run that length, and it's a grueling three-and-a-half-hour slog on a "dreary" commuter road with rush-hour cars and trucks speeding past. Murakami keeps track of the roadkill he encounters: a depressing total of three dogs and eleven cats. As he runs, he struggles with the heat, the wind, his thirst, and his own hatred of everyone and everything, including the sheep by the side of the road. But he finishes.

When we leave Murakami at the end of the book, he's run many more marathons, and even competed in his first triathlon. And of course he's still writing. And, one presumes, napping.

But all the descriptions of running and writing and training are both story and metaphor and, as Murakami somewhat sheepishly admits, the book "does contain a certain amount of what might be dubbed life lessons."

I read Murakami's book on running while I was lying fully clothed on my bed on top of my covers one hot summer day, preparing to take a nap. But the book was too fascinating to allow me to sleep, and I underlined furiously. The book is indeed full of life lessons. One has to do with knowing when to end a day's work: In running and writing, Murakami realizes, there is a real benefit to stopping before, and not after, you find yourself depleted. "Do that," he writes, "and the next day's work goes surprisingly smoothly. I think Ernest Hemingway did something like that. To keep on going, you have to keep up the rhythm. This is the important thing for long-term projects." I underlined the next sentence: "Once you set the pace, the rest will follow."

A few pages later, I underscored the observation, "I don't know why, but the older you get, the busier you become." Later Murakami writes about the need, as you get older, to prioritize your life. When he was young, he had endless time for everyone—he and his wife owned and ran a small bar back then. Now, though, he needs to ration whom he sees and what he does.

Still, he's careful to mention that even when he owned the bar, he never worried about pleasing everyone. If ten people came and nine of them didn't care for his bar, that didn't matter at all. He just needed one in ten to like it—well, to love it, to come back and be a regular. In order to make sure of that, he explains, "I had to make my philosophy and stance clear-cut, and patiently maintain that stance no matter what."

So it was with his books. Some readers may not have liked his first two novels, but he stuck with writing until the explosive success of *A Wild Sheep Chase*. He had to build an audience of people who loved what he did, to cultivate "devoted readers, the one-in-ten repeaters."

While reading this book in bed, I found myself thinking about Murakami's "life lessons," but I kept returning to the bit about napping. It's ironic, I know, to read a whole book about running, and to come away thinking mostly about one paragraph on sleep. But the more time I spent lying in bed pondering Murakami's book, the more I came to see the parallels between the two.

Murakami doesn't have a clue what he thinks about when

he runs but instead describes the thoughts that go through his head when he is running as being like clouds: "Clouds of all different sizes. They come and they go, while the sky remains the same sky as always. The clouds are mere guests in the sky that pass away and vanish, leaving behind the sky. The sky both exists and doesn't exist. It has substance and at the same time doesn't. And we merely accept that vast expanse and drink it in."

When I nap I may dream, and may even remember some of those dreams vividly, but the balance of my sleeping thoughts are also like clouds, images that "pass away and vanish."

Murakami relies on the quiet time of running, the time by himself, to maintain his "mental well-being" as well as his physical well-being, which gives him the stamina to keep doing what he does: sitting down to write and focusing on his work.

Napping, too, is a form of withdrawing. You may nap next to someone, but you nap alone—just as you can run alongside others, but you run by yourself. And napping, like running, produces a dream state—a trance, an out-of-body experience of the type that many chase through drugs and raves but that for the lucky are as near as the road or the bed.

Napping also has benefits that running doesn't.

The greatest thing about a nap is that it gives you two days for the price of one. You have the whole day before the nap, and when you wake up you have a whole day ahead of you.

For me, a perfect weekend day begins with a careful reading of the newspaper in the morning; an early lunch, perhaps with a Bloody Mary, if someone insists; then time with a book. After about forty minutes or so, my eyelids usually grow heavy and the book heavier. So I will certainly doze off.

Reading and naps, two of life's greatest pleasures, go especially well together. The best thing about a nap that interrupts my reading is that it often enriches my experience of a book by allowing my subconscious to place me in it. During these naps I might find myself galloping across the moors with Heathcliff or spending Mondays and Wednesdays with Morrie. When I wake, an hour or so later, I find the book I was reading splayed open on my chest with a new chapter lodged in my brain. I have all the benefits of time without thought and some new scenes and images as well.

If it's really a good day I can return to the book for another hour or so. Then I'll get up, splash some cold water on my face, and take care of some emails or pay some bills until 6:00 p.m., when it's time for a drink. All week I dream about just this kind of Saturday and Sunday.

I cherish memories of great naps—from my childhood, at my grandmother's house, resting my head on a needlepoint pillow that said BLESS THIS MESS, and from just days ago.

Sadly, we live in a world that is increasingly intolerant of naps and nappers.

In school, I perfected the art of the in-lecture nap, accomplished by placing my elbows on the desk, lacing my fingers together, and then cradling my head between my thumbs as though deep in concentration—but it's tough to get away with even this kind of nap in a cubicle or at a shared desk. Colleagues and bosses now expect to hear a certain amount of the key-tapping that has become consonant with work. Screens are programmed to sleep, as are computers, if they aren't fed a steady diet of numbers and letters by keyboard. And nothing betrays a sleeping worker like a sleeping computer. Ironic that we program our computers to do something that we now deny ourselves.

When there were offices, life for nappers was easier. The open-plan office, with everyone in constant sight of everyone else, is a disaster. So off we go to the break room again and again for coffee, that enemy of sleep, or for a quick trip to Starbucks for a sugar- and fat-filled specialty drink to keep us awake until the commute home.

Following Lin Yutang, I can't help myself from seeing napping, like lounging in bed awake, not just as a human pleasure but as a human right. The freedom to nap or lounge isn't quite one of Franklin Roosevelt's Four Freedoms (as enshrined by Eleanor Roosevelt in the Universal Declaration of Human Rights), but maybe it should be the fifth. (Eleanor was, by the way, known to take a power nap prior to giving speeches; Sir Winston Churchill was a great napper, too.)

There are scientific journals full of research on the physical benefits of naps, but none of that interests me. Researching napping is antithetical to the spirit of napping. Murakami, I believe, feels similarly. He mentions the health benefits of taking a nap but follows with the simple admission that he's always loved napping. You don't need a reason to do what you do for love.

I recently read a moving article by Toby Campbell, MD, a cancer oncologist who works in hospice and palliative care. He wrote an essay for the *Journal of the American Medical Association* about how he realized one sunny Wisconsin day that he "had bucket lists all wrong" and that his thinking about what was most important at the end of life needed to evolve. He was visiting a patient named Keith, who had been discharged from the hospital to home hospice with the expectation that he had days to live. But Keith was still alive three months later, though his family had reported that he was now "struggling." Hence the house-call from Dr. Campbell. Keith's family and friends had rallied around him—first with one celebration of his life and then, when he didn't die, with another celebration, and then, when he still didn't die, a third celebration. Keith was definitely dying—there was no doubt about that—just not as quickly as everyone had expected. Now, he was exhausted, he confided in Dr. Campbell, and not just because of his illness. The problem was that everyone around him was trying so hard to make every moment he had left meaningful that he didn't have a minute to himself.

Dr. Campbell realized that even though he had cared for many hundreds of people who were dying, his thoughts about the end of life might be misguided: "A continuously intense life can be exhausting. Keith had no bucket list of activities to complete before he died. He longed for a minute that didn't matter: perhaps for time to take a nap or watch something silly on television without feeling guilt or regret. He needed relief from the feeling that he was wasting precious time, not the added pressure of life's greatest to-do list. I now realize that humans require down time. Quiet time is necessary to process all that happens to us on a daily basis— let alone over the course of a life."

Of course, napping is also a privilege. My friends with children and multiple jobs rarely find themselves with time for a nap. But that's what makes napping that much sweeter for them when they do.

A few years back, I was on a business trip to a town where a friend lived. He picked me up after my meeting, and back we went to his apartment. We had lots to catch up on and much to chat about—it had been months since we had seen each other, and there was that pleasurable giddiness that comes when you have so many topics from which to choose and can alight on this one and that one. Your friends in common? Family? Your ailments? Books and movies?

Soon our conversation turned, as it so often does, to how busy life is. And my friend asked, "Would you like a nap?"

In fact I was desperate for a nap. I had flown in early. I had been worried about my business. The meeting had been stressful.

So he left me for twenty minutes to stretch out on the sofa and close my eyes. He went to the kitchen to send some emails.

"Would you like a nap?" is one of those questions we

should ask of one another more often. It's easy. And it costs exactly nothing.

The Importance of Living includes a section called "The Importance of Loafing." Here Lin Yutang writes about the horrors of "efficiency, punctuality and the desire for achievement and success." He calls them "Three American Vices." He writes, "They are the things that make the Americans so unhappy and so nervous. They steal from them their inalienable right of loafing and cheat them of many a good, idle and beautiful afternoon."

Happily, these three vices can be kept at bay very simply: Whenever you have the chance, you lie down on your bed and close your eyes.

Giovanni's Room
Connecting

I WALKED INTO the library. My palms were sweating. Not because I was nervous about anything specific, but because at sixteen my palms were always sweating. They were permanently clammy. Just as my face was permanently spotty, studded with angry pimples in various shades of pink and red. My hair was floppy and loose and covered my eyes. I'd finally saved enough money to dump my thick plastic glasses for a cooler pair—dark and round, like the ones John Lennon had. But my palms betrayed my efforts to be cool.

It was a warm day, and all the other kids were out playing sports or pretending to study or listening to the Grateful Dead or smoking in the woods. I was the only one at the library. And I wasn't sure what I hoped to find.

The library was a squat, stone building on a pond. Even without the air-conditioning turned on, it was always cool. The foyer held the card catalog and the desk of Miss Locke, the librarian. Past that was a grand reading room, with leather chairs and brass lamps. Beyond that, to the left, right, and center, were open stacks, with study carrels. There were more of these on the second floor, and a whole floor of open stacks below.

Though I would not have admitted it to myself, I was hoping to find Miss Locke at her desk. She always had the most amazingly delicious chocolate-chip brown-sugar brownies. She also always had a kind word for me—a funny, sly one, something that told me that we were on the same side, that we understood things others didn't.

But today she wasn't there. So I wandered around. I visited some of my favorite sections. I stopped by poetry, where I pulled from the shelf the collected works of Robert Frost. I went by drama, and pulled William Inge from the shelf, so I could flip to *The Dark at the Top of the Stairs* and revisit the monologue that always broke my heart, in which the boy, soon to die from suicide, remembers the time he was able to leave military academy to spend two whole days with his mother, and how he took her to dinner, out dancing, and to a show.

I was actually quite an outgoing kid, and I enjoyed the company of others. I knew this business of hanging out in the library and pulling favorite books from the shelves that had nothing to do with homework would make me seem aloof and pretentious and would puzzle most of my peers, so I kept it to myself.

And then I noticed the library cart, the one Miss Locke wheeled around as she returned to the shelves the books that kids had borrowed, or had simply taken down and then left out, like dirty dishes on a table, waiting for someone else to attend to them.

On the cart was a book. Just one book: *The Little That Is All* by John Ciardi. I picked it up and read the back of the book, which told me that this poet had "over the past thirty-odd years brought out ten volumes of poetry, a complete translation of Dante's *Divine Comedy*, a collection of his columns, *Manner of Speaking*, with numerous volumes of children's verse." Ciardi had become famous in the late 1960s and early 1970s, when poets were still famous.

I read some pages at random and then checked it out. It was not verse for children.

The poems spoke to me in a way that I think I would have found hard to explain, if I had attempted to do so, which I didn't.

There was one about washing your own feet. It includes the line "Washing my feet, I think of immortal toenails." I instantly loved that poem.

A poem called "East Sixty-Seventh Street" about the poet Frank O'Hara's death had a phrase that stuck with me: "suffering not to suffer / but because we are what we are and some of it hurts."

Most of all I loved "A Poem for Benn's Graduation from High School." Its last stanza reads: ". . . It does not, finally, / take much saying. There has even been time / to imagine we have said 'Goddamn it, I love you,' / and to hear ourselves saying it, and to pause / to be terrified by *that* thought and its possibilities."

I memorized as many poems as I could.

When I returned the book the next week, again I missed Miss Locke and her famous brownies. But again I found one book on the cart.

I wish I could remember what that book was, but I can't. What I do remember is that the next time I went I did find Miss Locke there, and we talked at greater length than we ever had before, and from then on I would tell her what I was reading, often a book from the cart, but she would never acknowledge that she'd left anything there specifically for me. Sometimes in these conversations she would recommend a book to me. The books she suggested were usually vaguely apt, the kinds of books she suggested to lots of kids, books that most people my age at that school seemed to like. But the ones I found on the cart were different. They were books, I believed, that spoke directly and peculiarly to me. Sometimes they were books that you wouldn't normally recommend to a young man in the 1970s at a boarding school, like *The Loom of Youth* by Alec Waugh, brother of Evelyn, who made his name with this novel of a gay scandal at a British public school. Sometimes they were books of poetry, always very accessible, but not what everyone else was reading, not Frost, not e e cummings, but more volumes of Ciardi, and Marianne Moore, and H.D. Once it was, surprisingly, *Our Bodies, Ourselves*, that life-changing bible for liberated 1970s women. On reflection, maybe that wasn't left on the cart for me.

It was a parallel curriculum to the one I was studying in my formal classes. And there was no particular thread—the works jumped around genre and history. But I believe that

(*Our Bodies, Ourselves* aside) they were selected for me and only me.

Of course, Miss Locke must have realized that I was gay a short time after I finally began to fully admit it to myself. Nobody but a gay boy obsessively rereads the monologue from *The Dark at the Top of the Stairs* or any plays by William Inge—or really any plays at all, for that matter. Not at an Episcopal boarding school in the 1970s. And nobody but a gay boy attempts *Marius the Epicurean* by Walter Pater, a book so stultifying it's impossible to imagine anyone today getting through it. The only reason I even knew about it was because I had started reading everything I could about Oscar Wilde, including *Son of Oscar Wilde* by Vyvyan Holland, the second of his two boys, who were whisked off to Continental Europe after their father was arrested. *Marius the Epicurean* was a book Wilde dearly loved by a professor who had a deep influence on him. So I read it.

But, again, this was the 1970s. So I didn't talk to anyone about Wilde or about my being gay. And Miss Locke didn't talk about it. She just left books for me.

Eventually she would leave for me Gore Vidal's gay novel *The City and the Pillar* and *Giovanni's Room* by James Baldwin, the 1956 novel about the love between two men: one American and one Italian. It's narrated by David, the American, on the eve of Giovanni's execution for murder—and tells in flashbacks its story of love, betrayal, and jealousy. The title refers to Giovanni's one-room apartment in Paris, a place where he and David were for a time happy together.

I wept extravagantly over *Giovanni's Room*, for Giovanni and for David. I was a dramatic fellow. Maybe that was my nature—and maybe it also came from all those afternoons in the school library reading William Inge and Oscar Wilde and the plays of Tennessee Williams. But even at my most self-absorbed, I was aware that, except with regard to being gay, my life wasn't very similar to the lives of either of the characters in that book, or to Baldwin's.

And yet having that gay thing in common was still something. It was a time of high stakes when it came to being gay. That year, Harvey Milk, the first openly gay elected official in America, was gunned down, along with San Francisco's mayor; their killer would receive a sentence of just seven years, of which he would serve five, after his attorneys argued that his mental state was caused by eating too many Twinkies. The previous year, Anita Bryant had launched a vicious national crusade against lesbian and gay people that was enthusiastically embraced by millions. There were no gay characters on television or in mainstream movies, save for ones who wound up killing themselves or someone else. Discrimination of all sorts was totally legal, nationwide, and would be for decades to come. Gay, lesbian, and transgender people were publicly reviled, with the threat of violence always present. (Of course, many forms of legal discrimination are still intact to this day, and the United States can be a dangerous place for LGBT people, especially for transgender women of color.)

At my school, there had never been, as far as I knew, a

single openly gay person in the student body or on the faculty. I believed that if anyone found out I was gay I would have to leave the school I loved.

It would certainly be too dramatic to say that the books Miss Locke left for me saved my life. But it has become clearer and clearer that these books helped me create a vision of a life that I could look forward to with something other than dread.

Baldwin writes, in the voice of his American character, David:

> Giovanni had awakened an itch, had released a gnaw in me. I realized it one afternoon, when I was taking him to work via the Boulevard Montparnasse. We had bought a kilo of cherries and we were eating them as we walked along. We were both insufferably childish and high-spirited that afternoon and the spectacle we presented, two grown men jostling each other on the wide sidewalk and aiming the cherry pits, as though they were spitballs, into each other's faces, must have been outrageous. And I realized that such childishness was fantastic at my age and the happiness out of which it sprang yet more so; for that moment I really loved Giovanni, who had never seemed more beautiful than he was that afternoon.

The life Baldwin promised in that one passage was something extraordinary. I didn't have to imagine a life where I could live like that; Baldwin had imagined it for me. And even the grim words and scenes that follow didn't diminish for me the magic of that promise.

Shortly after reading *Giovanni's Room*, I would come across a quote from Baldwin:

> You think your pain and your heartbreak are unprecedented in the history of the world, but then you read. It was books that taught me that the things that tormented me most were the very things that connected me with all the people who were alive, or who had ever been alive.

I would continue to read books by Baldwin, including *The Fire Next Time*, and the essay it contained about racism in America and American history written by the then thirty-nine-year-old African American author as a letter to his fourteen-year-old nephew. Reading this book, I felt horrified, saddened, complacent, and complicit. I still do. And rereading *Giovanni's Room* as an adult helped me see that book in a much-richer light—as an exploration of masculinity in its many forms and as a meditation on lies, shame, and grief.

Miss Locke introduced me to James Baldwin. And James Baldwin made me see myself and the world differently. He still does.

After graduating, when I would visit my school over anniversary weekends, I would stop by and say hello to Miss Locke. Legend was that she remembered every student; it's impossible to prove, but I've never met a student who says she didn't.

Over the years her hair changed from brown to gray, but

it was always immaculately waved. She wore the same kinds of sweater sets she always wore, favoring pastels. She spoke softly with the slightly nasal, broad-voweled accent of New Hampshire. And she always had a supply on hand of those pan-baked brownies. Kids continued to come to the library for these, which gave her the chance to put books in the path of those who might not otherwise seek them out.

During those visits we talked about the school, about faculty who had come and gone, and always about books we were reading. But our conversations weren't long, as the weekends were busy, and there were always other alums waiting for their chance to see Miss Locke.

I hope I thanked her. But I can't imagine I ever thanked her enough.

Miss Locke died in 2012 at age eighty-one, of ALS, Lou Gehrig's disease.

I learned from her obituary that she had started at my school as an assistant librarian in 1963. She retired in 1995, fifteen years after my graduation. She left behind adoring nieces and a nephew and grandnieces and grandnephews. I knew about many of them, because she talked about them with immense pride. She also left behind thousands of students for whom she had provided, always, the perfect word, hug, and book, whether handed to us directly, recommended, or left on a cart.

David Copperfield
Remembering

DICKENS FAMOUSLY SAID of *David Copperfield*, "Of all my books, I like this the best." It's easy to see why: the protagonist's childhood closely mirrors Dickens's—with its grim factory labor and privations. And he wrote it after the long illness and death of his beloved sister, which provided inspiration for the pivotal scene in the novel: the long illness and death of Copperfield's beloved Dora. (Almost nothing reduces me to a puddle of tears more quickly than reading that scene.)

The first time I read *David Copperfield*, it was summer and I was a young teen, staying with my grandmother in Westport, Connecticut. I adored Gran, but she wasn't an easy person, and she spent most of the day on a La-Z-Boy recliner, drinking white wine and watching golf. So I sat outside and read. From the first lines of *David Copperfield*, I was captivated: "Whether I shall turn out to be the hero of my own life, or whether that station will be held by anybody else, these pages must show." For several weeks, I was alone with

Gran. While I was reading this miracle of a book, David and Emily (aka Little Em'ly) and Dora were my friends.

And then there was Steerforth, the charismatic older schoolboy who takes young David under his wing. Dickens describes him as a "handsome boy"—and David Copperfield is totally smitten with him. I was, too. After Steerforth's first introduction in the book, the chapter ends with David staring at Steerforth as he sleeps. Steerforth brings about a turn in David's life and fortunes. And even though he later proves himself to be a bit of a rotter (especially with regard to how he treats Emily), there would be no David Copperfield without him—he saves David. So when I look back on the book, I rarely think of Steerforth's caddishness and treachery. What I recall instead is the way he adopted David and the bond between them when David needed him most. I have forgiven him, just as David Copperfield did.

After I turned the last page that long-ago summer, I sobbed even harder than I had when Dora died—mostly because I was going to miss these characters so much.

When I was writing the book about my mother and her death, several of my friends asked me if I was hoping that the book would give me "closure." What I realized was that I didn't want closure—I wanted to continue our conversations. Just because someone is gone doesn't mean that person exits your life. I remember vividly the day during that hot summer when I finished *David Copperfield*. But my engagement with David and Little Emily and Steerforth and Dora didn't end then—it had just begun. I talk to them and live with them. Just as I still talk to my mother.

I don't miss the characters in *David Copperfield* as much as I thought I would—because I never had to say goodbye. The characters never left me nor I them. *David Copperfield* stays with me to this day: David Copperfield himself, and also as he is refracted in the other Davids I have known.

There has been something very mysterious about the role that Davids have played in my life. Now, granted, David was a popular name around fifty years ago, the second most popular. We had four Davids in my grade-school class. I was the only Will. Still, I am not willing to cede all of this to demographics or happenstance.

My first best friend is named David. We met at kindergarten, were inseparable through school, slept over alternate Saturday nights at each other's houses for years, went to summer camp together, and have stayed in constant contact ever since. He and his wife made me the godfather of one of his children, and they named another after me. We live on different coasts, but there is nothing important in my life that I wouldn't need to tell them the day it happened.

I wrote a book about email with a friend named David.

My husband is named David.

And then there is David Baer. I met him sometime in September 1980 when we were college freshmen. We were in adjoining suites. I liked my suite mates but didn't connect deeply with any of them. We were a mismatched set, or that's how it seemed to me. David was in the same situation. And so we found each other.

Now, thanks to our endless photo taking and posting and updating, we may in years to come be able to find a record of the actual moment when we first met the people who would be most important to us, the people who would change our lives. Generations previous to mine were better diarists, so people of centuries past were able to do this, inasmuch as they captured first impressions in print. But I just have my creaky memory. So I can't say I remember the day I met David Baer.

I do remember, though, that when the president of the university addressed the freshman class on one of our first days, he mentioned that one of us was just sixteen, and when I first met David, I was sure he was the sixteen-year-old. He was several inches shorter than I was—so he couldn't have been more than five foot five. He was thin and wiry, with olive skin, unruly black hair, and a square jaw that he cocked to one side when he was thinking. I don't know if I asked him outright, but I soon discovered that he was my age. I never did find out who the sixteen-year-old was.

We became friendly, and then friends, and then great friends, and then roommates (sharing a suite with an incredibly good-natured drummer from Rumson, New Jersey, whom we referred to as Bamm-Bamm, both for the drumming and because in his exuberance he reminded us of Pebbles's sidekick in *The Flintstones*). David seemed profoundly East Coast—dark, Jewish, somewhat cynical, intense. But he was from Los Angeles; from a place above Santa Monica called Rustic Canyon that was, indeed, exactly that.

I would meet David's parents before too long—his mother, a school principal, and his father, a physicist who worked at the RAND Corporation. And eventually I met his twin brother. They looked only vaguely alike to me—though others couldn't tell them apart. Of the many differences between them, one seemed particularly important at that stage of our lives: David was gay and his brother straight.

David and I loved almost all the same things, but often for different reasons. So we always had more to talk about than the hours allowed. We both felt that Cyndi Lauper would outlast and outshine Madonna, but for David that was because of Lauper's haunting voice, and for me it was her superior lyrics. We loved a local pizza place called Naples, but David ordered the cinnamon toast, and I always had a slice. We loved the Francis Ford Coppola film of S. E. Hinton's *The Outsiders*, but for David that was because of Patrick Swayze, and I was all about Matt Dillon.

When it came to books, it was the same. We were both crazy about works by Christopher Isherwood. But David's favorite was the novel *A Single Man*, and I was most obsessed with Isherwood's memoir, *Christopher and His Kind*. David Baer also loved *David Copperfield*, and for the same initial reason—the friendship of Steerforth and our young protagonist. But he was among those who found Dora's death overwrought, whereas it continued to slay me. As I said, he had a cynical side—and that's a hard scene for anyone to stomach who looks at the world with a critical eye. He didn't love Dora the way I did—he found her unbearably silly and a bit cloying in her love for her husband. We were both, however, in full agreement about Emily; we loved her fervently and unreservedly.

After we graduated, I moved to Hong Kong. (On a whim, I had applied for a fellowship to study and teach there but had failed to get it; so on a bigger whim, I decided to go there under my own steam to try to be a journalist, having saved up enough money for a one-way ticket after months of work as a temporary secretary.) David Baer moved to New York to be near his boyfriend, to work for an architect, to save money for architecture school, and to savor the city he had come to love. This was before the Internet, so we wrote each other postcards and letters. But so much was happening for David in New York that even long letters couldn't contain it all. He had begun to make area "rugs" out of remnants of linoleum from the 1950s, and they caught on enough to be written up in the papers. He was hanging out with writers and painters on New York's Lower East Side, just as the art scene there was exploding with graffiti artists. He promised me he would come visit—when he saved up some money, when life slowed down a bit, when his applications were done. We had traveled together famously for a few weeks after our sophomore year and also when I had to come home to renew my six-month Hong Kong work visa. We would travel together again, we promised each other—this time throughout Asia, on the cheap.

And then one day, in 1986, in Hong Kong, I woke up feeling extraordinarily well. It was a Saturday. I went about my errands. Came back to my apartment. Tried to do some writing. I remember the most curious thing: one second I was feeling absolutely fine, better than fine, great, in fact.

And then the next second I was burning up. I thought I was going to vomit or pass out. I reached for a thermometer—my fever was 104. Then I broke out into a sweat, the proverbial cold sweat that people mention. I was shaking; sweat poured down my face; my clothes were drenched. And then I was fine, albeit weak and a bit wobbly. So I lay down for a nap only to be awoken some hours later by my brother, calling from New York to tell me that David Baer had been riding his bicycle to work when he hit a pothole in the street and lost control of the bicycle and slid under a bus right outside Lincoln Center and had been instantly killed. A mutual friend had tried to reach me and had found my brother instead. I would soon learn that David's father was on a plane to New York to see him, after a business trip, and would only find out about his son's death hours after my brother and I had spoken.

I'm not a believer in psychic phenomena. But as near as I can figure out, my fever had spiked for no reason at the exact moment David died.

I flew back home to New York from Hong Kong for the service. On the plane I wanted a whiskey. Northwest Airlines was charging four dollars, and I only had a twenty, and the flight attendant wouldn't make change. When I saw him collect dozens of singles from the two dollars they were charging for headsets, I asked him again to make change. He wouldn't. That was the headset money. He couldn't use it to make change for drinks. In that moment, on the edge of rage, I was overwhelmed by the full misery of David's death.

Suddenly, I missed David Baer so much that I wasn't sure I was going to be able to stand it. I was sadder and angrier than I had ever been and knew that if I started to express it I wouldn't be able to stop.

I counted from one to ten again and again and again and again until I finally fell asleep.

At the funeral, I was in a daze, as was everyone. I was also jet-lagged. I realized then that grief and jet lag have much in common—the world isn't spinning right, you can't sleep, or you are exhausted and then wide-awake, you feel dizzy and feverish and ill. Hot one minute; cold the next. More than anything, you feel strange and unmoored and displaced. It's a leap of faith to believe you will ever feel any different, ever feel the same. With jet lag you soon recover fully; with grief you don't. Jet lag quickly ends; grief can get worse before it gets better, if it does.

When David Copperfield loses his wife, Dora, he thinks:

> This is not the time at which I am to enter on the state of
> my mind beneath its load of sorrow. I came to think that
> the Future was walled up before me, that the energy and
> action of my life were at an end, that I never could find any
> refuge but in the grave. I came to think so, I say, but not in
> the first shock of my grief. It slowly grew to that.

When I lost David Baer, I couldn't actually believe at first that he was gone. I kept expecting him to turn up, the way characters do in Dickens, chapters later. But as time went by,

I finally accustomed myself to a world without him. It's not the same world. It never will be.

I also went through a period of intense guilt. He had been thinking about coming to visit me in Hong Kong. Why didn't I *insist* he come? If he had been in Hong Kong, he wouldn't have been in New York riding a bicycle that day, and he would still be alive. I knew this was irrational, but it was much easier to blame myself than no one.

What kind of impression can someone make in five years? Sadly and happily I know the answer to that question. Deep. Cavernous. I can't say I think about David Baer every day. But I do think about him many days. And those days are usually happy. It's when several days have gone by and I realize that I haven't thought of him that I feel his loss most acutely.

I love to talk about David—with our friends, with his boyfriend—and I love to tell others about him. Usually this makes me happy, but sometimes all I can think about is how much I miss him.

Someone once told me that when he is intensely missing someone who has died, he makes up a little story in his mind. For example, he'll decide that a dead friend is actually just working at a salmon cannery in Alaska, and that it's very remote, and there's no phone or Internet. When I miss David too much, I like to think of him at a cannery or on a boat or a tropical island. He'll be home soon, and I'll see him then.

After the memorial service, David's parents wanted me to have something of his. They gave me several of his drawings and also a copy of his thesis, on John Ruskin, the nineteenth-century British artist and critic. It was an attempt to explain how Ruskin's views of nature changed the way we view nature. It brought together literature and art and architecture.

On my bookshelf I keep a volume of John Ruskin and a copy of *David Copperfield*, and I visit them whenever I've gone too long without remembering my beautiful, vibrant friend, who like Dora died way too young.

Last year I met a hospice worker. He was telling me that he loved his work with dying people and their families and constantly looked to literature for wisdom for himself and to share. He showed me a notebook full of quotes, words he had come across and kept close at hand. As I was flipping through, I noticed one from John Ruskin: "When I have been unhappy, I have heard an opera from end to end, and it seemed the shrieking of winds; when I am happy, a sparrow's chirp is delicious to me. But it is not the chirp that makes me happy, but I that makes *it* sweet."

When I think of David Baer, I get to choose whether remembering him makes me sad or happy, whether I remember his death or his life. I try to choose happy. I try to choose life.

Wonder
Choosing Kindness

Wonder, a novel by R. J. Palacio about a boy who is just about to start fifth grade, makes me want to be a better person. I want to tell you about it—but first I'm going to obsess a little about my weight.

Every January I used to buy a slew of diet books, and I would read them right away, convinced that this would be the year I would finally lose some pounds.

I would do pretty well for a while on a diet of skinless, boneless chicken breasts and water. But then the doughnuts and beer would come back, and the weight along with them. I would beat myself up a bit, but then move on, vowing to do better next year. Not tomorrow or next month: next year. Having blown my New Year's resolutions, I could now wait another eleven months before getting serious.

Of course, some of these diet books were worse than others. The grapefruit diet books were never going to work, no matter how religiously I followed them. Man cannot live on grapefruit (and protein, also allowed) alone. But some were good—in fact, excellent—with sensible advice, clear logic, and realistic strategies. If I followed the advice in those books, I could change, and change for good. So why did I find it so hard to follow sound advice?

Other books I've read, books like Charles Duhigg's *The Power of Habit*, explain why I'm failing to change my habits and how I might succeed. Duhigg presents studies that show you need to recognize cues and institute a system of rewards to change a bad habit (gorging on chocolates after dinner, spending too much money on magazines I barely read, wasting time on the Internet) or to institute a good one (going to the gym to do cardio). I had never allowed myself sufficient time nor given myself rewards along the way.

We buy self-help books and read them because they encourage us to believe that we can change—that we can become slimmer, healthier, richer, better versions of ourselves. Books can help us figure out who we want to be. And that's not a small thing. But this habit changing is a tough business. And I suppose that if any of these books could work magic without considerable effort, then that would be the end of that category of book. The foolproof diet book would be the last diet book anyone would ever need to publish.

To further complicate matters, most of us read for escape *and* instruction. And yet when we wander into the self-help, business, psychology, and diet sections of the bookstore, we generally tell ourselves we are interested *only* in instruction. But is this really true? Perhaps simply flipping through a book advocating a grapefruit diet (and gazing at its glossy grapefruit pictures) will make me feel thinner—if only for the subway ride home. Viewed in that light, was my annual pilgrimage to buy diet books really something to regret? The only thing wrong with this habit was that I didn't examine my motives closely enough; I mistook escape for a desire to change.

At the same time, some of us also look to the fiction section to feel inspired to do better. I read novels in part because they help me figure out who I want to be. In a standard-issue police procedural, say, I want to be more like the detective and less like the killer. In a subtler work, though, I may find myself comparing my behavior with that of a number of different characters simultaneously or being drawn to a certain aspect of someone's character while remaining wary of another. Rereading Jane Austen's *Pride and Prejudice*, I want to mirror Elizabeth Bennet's strength and sense of duty, but I hope I'm not quite so quick to judge those around me as she is throughout most of the novel.

But much of fiction's effect is, I think, subliminal. It changes us even though we don't know we are being changed. Studies have shown that reading fiction makes us more empathetic. I would like to think that even with inconsistent effort on my part, I'm now less proud and prejudiced than I was when I first met Lizzy Bennet, even though I'm still plenty proud and prone to prejudice. (Must read again.)

There's the maxim that you can't judge a person until you've walked a mile in his or her shoes (or moccasins).

Certainly, fiction is one of the best ways to accomplish this. How else could you be on the front lines of revolution in eighteenth-century France *and* marooned on a Pacific island on a single flight home to JFK? I burned a lot of shoe leather with Jean Valjean fleeing Javert while reading Victor Hugo's *Les Misérables*. I was also racing alongside the heroic Ralph in William Golding's 1954 novel, *Lord of the Flies*, as he was running for his life through the burning jungle to escape his antagonist Jack and the other boys.

Still, if diet books tend to fill me with an unrealistic sense of hope about my ability to change, I find that fiction works in the opposite way; I often wonder whether, amid the chaos of revolution, I would behave the way Jean Valjean did or be much more like the relentless Javert—whether, if marooned, I would stand apart with Ralph and his tiny band or follow Jack and his feral crew.

Reading challenges you to figure out what kind of person you want to be. I'm going to call this the *Wonder* challenge, named for the book I mentioned and for the act of pondering this kind of question.

If you find the need to categorize books, you would consider *Wonder* a middle-grade reader; it was published and marketed for fourth- to sixth-graders who have graduated from simple chapter books but aren't ready for the darker themes of young adult. Written under the pseudonym R. J. Palacio by a successful book publisher and art director, the story is told from multiple perspectives, in a variety of voices. It centers on a young boy named August (Auggie), the first narrator, who has a craniofacial deformity. For years, Auggie has been tutored at home. Now, at the age of ten, he is about to start school for the first time.

I had picked it up to see if it might be good to recommend to my niece and nephews. Once I started, I couldn't stop reading. I desperately wanted Auggie to fit in at school, to be happy, to find friends—to have a place in his life other than his home where people could see him and not react in horror to his face.

At first, all goes much better for Auggie than I would have expected. But soon he encounters real cruelty and, what's worse, betrayal. The book's use of many narrators performs a double function: it both allows us to see what motivates people to behave the way that they do and also gives voice to our own fears and anxieties. It helps us reckon with how we might behave when faced with the same situation by coming at it in different ways. The author even followed *Wonder* with a book that includes the perspective of the classmate who bullies Auggie, the kid who calls him a freak and who tells other children that if they touch him they'll get the plague.

Much of the wisdom in the book comes from Auggie's teacher Mr. Browne, who is in the habit of sharing precepts with the class to help them learn how to deal with life's challenges and dilemmas. But it's the school's principal, Mr. Tushman, who, in his middle-school commencement address, sums up best the most important lesson of the year. His instruction to his students is both simple and arduous: Choose kindness. I was surprised and pleased to note that he explains kindness to the fifth- and sixth-graders with references to books. First, he cites a book by J. M. Barrie (not, he tells them, *Peter Pan*, but a book called *The Little White Bird*). He reads the sentence " 'Shall we make a new rule of life . . . always to try to be a little kinder than is necessary?' " He explains: "What a marvelous line, isn't it? Kinder than is *necessary*. Because it's not enough to be kind. One should be kinder than needed. Why I love that line, that concept, is that it reminds me that we carry with us, as human beings, not just the capacity to be kind, but the very choice of kindness."

Mr. Tushman then continues with a passage from a second book, Christopher Nolan's *Under the Eye of the Clock*. In this creatively structured memoir, Nolan tells in effervescent prose the story of his childhood and his education as a poet and writer. Born in Ireland in 1965 with cerebral palsy, Nolan was only able to control his eyes and his head. With the help of his father (who read to him great works of Irish and world literature) and his mother (who taught him the alphabet and talked to him constantly) and his sister, he first learned to communicate by signaling with his eyes and then began to use a pointer strapped onto his forehead like a unicorn horn to hit letters one at a time on a special computer keyboard. Nolan tells us that, with this setup and starting at age eleven, "he gimleted his words onto white sheets of life. Hands hanging loose by his side, electric pulses shooting through his body, he just nodded and nodded, typing numb-lost language" that had been trapped inside him for all his childhood years. Nolan would go on to compose remarkable and acclaimed poems, stories, plays, and a novel, and also to graduate from Trinity College, Dublin. He died at age forty-three in 2009.

Nolan's memoir was published in 1987, when he was twenty-two. He writes in the third person and calls himself Joseph.

Here's what Mr. Tushman says to the fifth- and sixth-graders:

". . . Ah, here we go. In *Under the Eye of the Clock*, by Christopher Nolan, the main character is a young man who is facing some extraordinary challenges. There's this one part where someone helps him: a kid in his class. On the surface, it's a small gesture. But to this young man, whose name is Joseph, it's . . . well, if you'll permit me . . ."

He cleared his throat and read from the book: " 'It was at moments such as these that Joseph recognized the face of God in human form. It glimmered in their kindness to him, it glowed in their keenness, it hinted in their caring, indeed it caressed in their gaze.' "

He paused and took off his reading glasses again.

"It glimmered in their kindness to him," he repeated, smiling. "Such a simple thing, kindness. Such a simple thing. A nice word of encouragement given when needed. An act of friendship. A passing smile."

What he wants them to understand is this: "If every single person in this room made it a rule that wherever you are, whenever you can, you will try to act a little kinder than is necessary—the world really would be a better place. And if you do this, if you act just a little kinder than is necessary, someone else, somewhere, someday, may recognize in you, in every single one of you, the face of God."

Mr. Tushman is careful to add that his listeners can replace "God" with "whatever politically correct spiritual representation of universal goodness you happen to believe in," which earns him smiles, laughter, and applause.

By the time we get to this portion of the book, so close to the end, we have seen terrible viciousness. But we've also seen the face of God (or whatever we call it) in Auggie, in the friends who stuck with him, in his family, and in some of the teachers at the school.

Choose kindness. Whenever there's a choice—and we are faced with such choices almost every minute of every day—this is what the book would have us remember.

Of course, no book can reform human nature, with all its flaws, just as no book will ever cause pounds to melt magically from our bodies. Even a book like *The Importance of Living*, with its advice that we need to be lazier and more sybaritic versions of our current selves, isn't so easy to follow. It takes discipline to try to relax and enjoy life a bit more.

Still, the union of imagination and action can be a powerful force. In fact, one of the lovely things about *Wonder* is that it sprang from the author's challenging herself to be kinder. In an interview with Michele Norris on National Public Radio, the author explained *Wonder*'s genesis: She was in an ice-cream store with her own children when one of them, then just three, burst into tears after he saw the face of a little girl with a facial deformity who was eating ice cream nearby. Palacio was so mortified that she grabbed her children and raced out the door. Afterward, she was furious that she hadn't managed the situation better: "What I should have done is simply turned to the little girl and started up a conversation and shown my kids that there was nothing to be afraid of," she told Norris. "And that got me thinking a lot about what it must be like to . . . have to face a world every day that doesn't know how to face you back."

Wonder's popularity spread in that most magical of ways: by word of mouth. Readers, booksellers, and librarians all started to recommend it to one another. Schools began to introduce it into the curriculum, and it became one of those books that a whole community decides to read together. In other words, it envisioned a possibility so intensely that it galvanized people to reproduce it in their lives and communities. Today it is well on its way to becoming one of the most beloved children's books of all time.

So the *Wonder* challenge after reading this book is to wonder if, in fact, we are choosing kindness—and to try to challenge ourselves to live more kindly.

Because clearly people can read this book, profess to love it, and then immediately and blatantly choose not to be kind. At the same time, I do hope that if we *are* inclined to be kind, a book like *Wonder* reminds us of that inclination. And if we aren't, then maybe it nudges us a bit in that direction.

Certainly, as this book has already proven, it can begin a conversation that helps us create safer communities for children and encourages us to hold one another to a slightly higher standard. Fiction doesn't exist to change us for the better; but I believe it almost always does. Fiction opens us up.

As for my annual flirtation with diet books and diets, I did finally manage to lose some of the weight I had been trying to lose for more than a decade, and I've kept most of it off for two years as of the time of this writing. It was a lot of work, and it involved a great deal more than simply reading a book; I had to create new habits and tangible rewards, just as Charles Duhigg had predicted I would. I had to get much more serious about the gym. I had to learn how to eat a lot better (and a lot less) and remember to walk a lot more. And I have to think about it every single day.

I'm still working on the kindness, and it's not as easily measured as weight and body fat. But I like to think that I'm getting a bit kinder every year and staying that way. And when I fall short, I often think of Auggie.

Lateral Thinking
Solving Problems

Lateral Thinking: An Introduction by Edward de Bono was first published in 1967, before the dawn of the personal computer revolution. This book does something more powerful than any computer: it helps you figure out solutions when you have the questions all wrong. There's no computer in the world that can give you the right output if you are giving it the wrong input.

The first computer I ever used was called the Kaypro II. It was a funny machine: one slice of it unclipped and exposed a keyboard within, leaving the main body of the computer exposed, displaying its floppy ports. You would stick in two floppy disks, and then it would do a mysterious activity it called "swapping." You typed a bit; it swapped a bit. You typed a bit more; it swapped a bit more. You had to wait for it. There was a little screen that glowed green and made you feel as if you were monitoring some wonky piece of equipment on a Cold War submarine.

But in the mid-1980s it was still amazing. You wrote and it saved what you wrote. And you could change it. And then, when you were really ready, you hooked it up to your dot-matrix printer, and magic would happen as—line by laborious line—it reproduced whatever it was you had so carefully written and revised.

Soon, however, frustration set in. Sometimes you could get in only a few words before the endless swapping began. There was nothing you could do while it was performing this mysterious procedure. You just had to wait for it to do its thing.

Often, it wouldn't stop, and you were faced with a dilemma—sit there and watch it endlessly swap, hoping it would finish; or reboot. To reboot, you had to kill the power. You either turned it off and then back on or unplugged it from the wall, waited, and plugged it back in. Rebooting was always a gamble. It gave you the immediate satisfaction of bringing the swapping to a close, but you didn't know what you would find when power was restored. At best, everything you had written to date was there with all the latest revisions. At worst, it was all gone. But often you found yourself in purgatory—after the reboot, the machine was still swapping.

I often think of that Kaypro in relation to a bad habit I have. It's my inability to disengage from a topic that is causing me anxiety. A friend told me that there's a psychological term for this—"perseverating." I thought she'd made it up, but then I discovered that there really is such a word.

My talent for perseverating is epic and usually fixes on a choice I've made that it's too late to change. The intensity of my perseveration has no connection to what's at stake. Should I take a 6:00 a.m. flight or an 8:00 a.m. flight? I'll choose the 6:00 a.m. (because it assures me of being at my destination in plenty of time), but then I'll perseverate for days over whether I've made an error. Will I be exhausted when I get there? I should have gone at 8:00 a.m. But then again, what if the 8:00 a.m. was delayed? Then I'd miss the event. But what if I oversleep and miss the 6:00 a.m.?

I have certain tricks to stop myself from perseverating. As I did with the Kaypro, I can attempt a reboot. This usually involves a sleeping pill. The hope is that if I go to sleep in the middle of a fit of perseveration, I'll wake up knowing the right choice or reconciled to the decision I've made or no longer concerned at all. Often this works. But often I'm like the purgatory version of the Kaypro—as soon as I'm awake I'm right back into the mental swapping, this or that, this or that.

Lateral Thinking often helps me snap out of it. I just need to remind myself to reread it.

Edward de Bono is a medical doctor, a psychologist, and a writer. Among his constant topics are creativity, language, and logic.

De Bono begins the book with the story of a merchant in debt. The banker who holds the debt wants to marry the merchant's daughter, against her will. He suggests a game of chance to determine her fate. They are standing on a "pebble-strewn path," pebbles everywhere, so the banker proposes that he place into a bag two pebbles: a white one and a black one. If the merchant's daughter draws the white one, she doesn't have to marry the banker and the debt is relieved. But if she draws the black one, then she must marry him. If she refuses to draw, then the merchant will go to debtor's prison.

They all agree. But the daughter notices that the banker has actually slipped two *black* pebbles into the bag, not a *black* and a *white*. If she draws, she can only get a black pebble and she will have to marry the banker. If she refuses, her father goes to jail. And if she tries to reveal the situation, she'll be accusing the banker of lying. He'll probably then cancel the whole idea of the game and send the father to debtor's prison, as is his right.

If you are a vertical thinker, Edward de Bono points out, those are the only choices.

Lateral thinkers, however, see other paths. They don't just work with the tools they are given, assuming that no other options exist. They challenge assumptions and find new tools.

The merchant's daughter is a lateral thinker. She draws a pebble, but before anyone can see what color it is, she drops it on the pebble-strewn path. Clumsy her. But by showing everyone that the pebble left in the bag is the black one, the only conclusion that can be drawn is that she chose the white. For the banker to dispute this, he would have to admit that he cheated. So the debt is discharged, and she's free to marry whomever she likes.

Another example comes from a parable in *The Jātaka (Stories of the Buddha's Former Births)*. Written originally in Pali, the sacred language of Buddhism, the parable tells the story of a young man with a golden complexion who has grown up in a forest hermitage, looking after his poor, blind parents. Over the course of his childhood, he has become friends with all the animals, but especially a golden deer, who helps him find streams so he can fetch water. One day, a king is out on a hunt and sees the golden boy with the golden deer and accidentally shoots the boy and not the deer with a poison arrow. The poisoned young man, slipping into a coma, asks the king to bring his parents so they can say goodbye to their dying son. When the couple reach their son, they are in complete despair, sobbing, believing that all is lost. But then, miraculously, Indra, the king of all celestial beings, appears in the sky. Indra announces to the blind couple that they can have any wish granted but only one wish. And Indra gives them three suggestions: the first, their sight returned; the second, their son restored to health; the third, a pot of gold. The couple confers briefly and then makes their one wish: "We want to see our healthy son carrying a bag of gold." Indra rewards their ingenuity: their son and their sight are restored—with money to last them the rest of their lives.

For Buddhists, this is a tale of effective speech. For me, lateral thinking.

Which flight should I take? The 6:00 a.m. that gets me up too early but assures my being there in time, even though I'll be exhausted? Or the 8:00 a.m., which is cutting it way too close? How about neither—how about I fly in late the night before, stay with a friend so I can catch up with her over breakfast (nice!), and be assured of arriving at my event well rested and on time?

De Bono believes we aren't born lateral thinkers; that we can train ourselves to think this way. Among the strategies he proposes, there's one I find particularly appealing: introducing truly random elements and ideas to force yourself to think differently about a problem you are facing. He calls it "random input." It can be as simple as opening a dictionary and putting your finger on the first word you find and trying to see if that helps you gain a new perspective. Anything that jolts you from your thinking rut.

And if we are searching for that random input, it can always come in the form of a book. Even one that doesn't seem the slightest bit relevant to the problem at hand: a novel or biography or book of poetry. The worst that can happen is we are still swapping, still perseverating, and still confused. But at least we've just read an interesting book.

Gift from the Sea
Recharging

WHEN I STARTED in book publishing, in 1987, after I returned from my three postcollege years working as a journalist and magazine editor in Hong Kong, I spent long hours at the office. I was never prompt in the morning, but I stayed late just about every night and worked just about every weekend. I didn't always work very efficiently. But I worked. It was a different time; we still used carbon paper to make copies of the letters we wrote, and only the executive secretaries were lucky enough to have IBM Selectric typewriters, with their magical rolling balls. The rest of us (from assistants like me all the way up to senior editors) made do with balky Smith Coronas, which had cartridges you would snap in and snap out when you needed to make corrections.

I was proud of how hard I worked. I was in my mid-twenties and was confident that no one logged more hours than I did.

One spring day, however, I had a conversation that greatly

changed my thoughts on work. It was with a formidable editor, one of the stars of the company. She was then in her fifties and was known for her editorial acumen and occasionally sharp tongue. But she seemed to like me, and we spoke often. In fact, I'd never seen evidence of the sharp tongue. I thought we were just chatting when she asked me how much time I was taking off that summer and if I was going to be able to afford to leave town for my holiday.

"I don't know if I'll be able to take a holiday this year," I told her. "I'm way too busy."

Suddenly, she became very severe. She fixed me with an icy glare and then said, "I thought better of you. But you're clearly either a megalomaniac or a fool." She paused. "You're a megalomaniac if you think we all can't survive for a few weeks without your contributions. And you're a fool if you think we can, but still insist on working through your vacation."

It was several days before she spoke warmly to me again. And when she did, I told her of my plan to visit a friend on the nearby Jersey Shore.

I thought of this conversation when I read Anne Morrow Lindbergh's classic book, *Gift from the Sea*.

This is one of those books I'd heard about and seen on countless shelves, especially in, predictably enough, beach cottages. The author was the widow of aviator Charles Lindbergh and the mother of the baby who had been so notoriously kidnapped and murdered in 1932.

In an introduction to the fiftieth-anniversary edition,

Anne Morrow Lindbergh's daughter Reeve writes of her mother:

> I remember how small and delicate she always seemed. I remember her intelligence and her sensitivity. But when I reread *Gift from the Sea*, the illusion of fragility falls away, leaving the truth. How could I forget? She was, after all, a woman who raised five children after tragically losing her first son in 1932. She was the first woman in America to earn a first-class glider pilot's license, in 1930, and the first woman ever to win the National Geographic Society's Hubbard Medal, in 1934, for her aviation and exploration adventures. She also received the National Book Award, in 1938, for *Listen! The Wind*, her novel based on those adventures, and she remained a best-selling author all her life.

Anne Morrow Lindbergh, even with all her published works, remains something of an enigma. This is especially true with regard to her noninterventionist stance in the early years of World War II. Her antiwar writings prior to the attack on Pearl Harbor may have been fueled by naive pacifism and the desire to support her husband. She would later express regret about what she called her ignorance and blindness with regard to Hitler and Nazi Germany.

Twenty-three years after the murder of her son and ten years after the end of World War II, Anne Morrow Lindbergh wrote *Gift from the Sea*. It became an immediate sensation, selling hundreds of thousands of copies in its first year and millions since. It has never been out of print.

Gift from the Sea is a quiet book of reflections and meditations written during and after a period of time spent at the Florida seashore. Each chapter takes its inspiration from a different shell the author finds along the beach. The book contains Lindbergh's thoughts on feminism, the environment, motherhood, marriage, work, love, independence, and, more broadly, how we manage our time and our lives.

Some of Lindbergh's advice comes across as dated. But most of it doesn't. Her words are directed toward other women, but most of her advice is for anyone who seeks to find balance in life.

The first gift from the sea is a channeled whelk shell. She is struck by the simplicity, bareness, and beauty of that shell. Her "shell" is not at all like that. She writes of the life in her house in the suburbs:

It involves food and shelter; meals, planning, marketing, bills and making the ends meet in a thousand ways. It involves not only the butcher, the baker, the candlestickmaker but countless other experts to keep my modern house with its modern "simplifications" (electricity, plumbing, refrigerator, gas-stove, oil-burner, dish-washer, radios, car and numerous other labor-saving devices) functioning properly. It involves health; doctors, dentists, appointments, medicine, cod-liver oil, vitamins, trips to the drugstore. It involves education, spiritual, intellectual, physical; schools, school conferences, car-pools, extra trips for basket-ball or orchestra practice; tutoring; camps, camp equipment and transportation. It involves clothes, shopping, laundry, cleaning, mending, letting skirts down and sewing buttons on, or finding someone else to do it. It involves friends, my husband's, my children's, my own, and endless arrangements to get together; letters, invitations, telephone calls and transportation hither and yon.

My husband and I have no children. We've never wanted children of our own, which is good because we can barely keep our one houseplant alive. But our friends who are parents tell me that this description of life fifty years ago almost exactly describes their lives today.

Lindbergh also writes about the challenges of "ever widening circles of contact and communication." She's referring to print media and radio—but she could easily be talking about Facebook and Twitter and Instagram as well: "What a circus act we women perform every day."

The problem as she sees it is "how to remain whole in the midst of the distractions of life."

The solution? Neither easy nor complete. She notes that it isn't possible to renounce life, to become a hermit, a nun. What she can do, she decides, is to establish an alternating rhythm between the clutter of her daily life and the simplicity she experiences at the beach and the beach house. She notes that, "for the most part, we, who could choose simplicity, choose complication." The gift of the whelk shell is the reminder to choose, whenever possible, simplicity.

The moon shell is another gift from the sea: this shell

reminds her of the importance of relearning to be alone and scheduling time alone. "The world today does not understand, in either man or woman, the need to be alone." She writes that if you say you have a business appointment scheduled, no one will try to convince you to break it to schedule something routine. "But if one says: I cannot come because that is my hour to be alone, one is considered rude, egotistical or strange." She is particularly adamant that women need solitude—and must find a way to get it, however they can.

Other shells bring her thoughts on love, relationships, and acceptance, silence, selectivity, significance, and beauty. The shell that brings her the gift of beauty is especially important to her.

She writes, "My life in Connecticut, I begin to realize, lacks this quality of significance and therefore of beauty, because there is so little empty space . . . Too many activities, and people, and things. Too many worthy activities, valuable things and interesting people. For it is not merely the trivial which clutters our lives but the important as well. We can have a surfeit of treasures—an excess of shells, where one or two would be significant."

An excess of shells is certainly a happy problem. But it is a problem nonetheless.

Her solution is surprising: to choose whenever possible the unknown over the familiar, for "it is the unknown with all its disappointments and surprises that is the most enriching."

As I am writing this, the world (including myself) is

caught up in a love affair with a book called *The Life-Changing Magic of Tidying Up* by Japanese home-organization guru Marie Kondo. The book instructs you to go through your home, category by category, not room by room or closet by closet. You lay out all your clothes on the floor; or all your books; or all your knickknacks. And then you hold up each item and ask yourself if it gives you joy. If it doesn't, out it goes. It's a technique that works, but works best for those who live alone. Several couples I know have been embroiled in ferocious arguments when one person decided that every single item laid out on the floor still gave joy and the other felt quite the opposite.

I've attempted to apply Kondo's advice. I've been very successful with my clothes, which is probably because I don't care very much about clothes. I've not been very successful with ridding myself of books. Most of my books give me joy. Even Bruce Lee's *Tao of Jeet Kune Do*, the manual for a martial art I will never practice. Even each one of my several coffee table books devoted to portraits of ornamental chickens. (Actually, those give joy to everyone who sees them.) And once a cookbook enters my home, it's never leaving.

Nor am I parting with Kondo's book. It gives me joy, too. Reading it allows me a vision of my life where we can set our mugs of tea on a table without having to clear a space for them; where our chest of drawers isn't crammed full of odds and ends; where we have eight plates that all match and not eleven sole survivors from previous sets and rummage sales.

I enjoy the Kondo fantasy. And it is indeed a pleasure to be able to find things easily in my now-somewhat-cleaner closet. And yet I'm pretty sure I wouldn't be any happier in the completely pristine version of my life than I am in its semi-messy present.

While Kondo gives techniques for ridding ourselves of physical clutter, Anne Morrow Lindbergh's book reminds us of all the other kinds of clutter that burden us. It also helps us forgive ourselves when we realize that jettisoning our emotional and spiritual clutter is more difficult than the very difficult task of throwing away all that stuff that no longer gives us joy.

The Taste of Country Cooking
Nourishing

EVERYONE THINKS our friend Marco Pasanella and his wife, Becky, and their son, Luca, are Italian, and everyone is both wrong and right. Marco was born in New York and grew up in New York; but his grandparents were Italian, and he spent a good part of his childhood there, mostly summers, especially after his father moved back to Italy when Marco was in college. So he's half-Italian, with dual citizenship. Becky is from rural Pennsylvania, but her sense of style and hospitality are pure Italy, a country she first visited and fell in love with as an adult, on trips to see her in-laws. And Luca, age ten, likes nothing more than to eat and hang out with friends. So, as far as I'm concerned, that makes them all Italian.

For years, the Italian government thought Marco was wholly Italian—and tried to conscript him for mandatory military service every time he came to visit. Eventually his age did what his father's attempts to fix the paperwork could not. When Marco turned forty, the Italian government ceased its efforts to enlist or imprison him, and finally ended all conscription two years later. But these bureaucratic troubles didn't lessen Marco's love for Italy, nor his father's. Marco's father loved Italy with all his heart: the art; the landscapes, which he painted every day right up to the day he died, age seventy-nine; and the food.

In his eulogy for his father, Marco mentioned that his father's last supper was a Christmas Day feast with friends in Torre del Lago, a lake town. Marco's father ate:

    Antipasto di pesce
    Risotto ai frutti di mare
    Branzino al forno
    Dolce
    Vino bianco

"I know this," Marco said, "because, for thirty-five years, my father kept a diary that listed everything he ate and drank and with whom. Twenty-five thousand two hundred fifty times, according to my calculations, he listed the dishes and the beverages along with a seating chart. Overlaid onto the meals are a series of color-coded lines and shapes, which I have yet to decipher. Other than the date, the menu, and the dining companions, there are no other words in his diary."

For Marco's father, I suspect the food diary did more than simply help him remember what he ate and with whom; I would guess it helped him remember everything else he did that day, his whole life.

A company in Silicon Valley is now manufacturing shakes called Soylent (an odd nod to a film called *Soylent Green* about—spoiler alert!—cannibalism). The idea is that you don't ever have to stop working—you can just suck down one of these shakes a few times a day and get all the nutrition you need.

Lin Yutang believed that nothing was more important than having meals with friends. In *The Importance of Living*, he writes, "It's a pretty crazy life when one eats in order to work and does not work in order to eat." Lin Yutang's wife and daughter believed the same; they devoted years of their lives to creating a book called *Chinese Gastronomy*, which helped introduce the world to real Chinese food.

I live to eat. I think about food all day long. By the time I finish dinner each evening, I'm already excitedly pondering what I'll eat the next morning, noon, and night.

Often, a novel I'm reading will make me ravenous. *Babette's Feast* by Isak Dinesen, *Like Water for Chocolate* by Laura Esquivel, *Sticks and Scones* by Diane Mott Davidson, *The Debt to Pleasure* by John Lanchester, and *The Book of Salt* by Monique Truong—I had to put each of these books down after a few chapters and run to the grocery store or a nearby restaurant. And it's not only from tales that feature food. Any story set in Japan, for example, will make me desperate for Japanese food. And any book set on the high seas will make me crave seafood, even *In the Heart of the Sea*, a work of nonfiction by Nathaniel Philbrick about the search for the real Moby-Dick, a book where the main source of sustenance for the sailors is, by necessity, other sailors. It didn't make me into a cannibal, but it did leave me with a fierce hunger for shrimp scampi.

And anyone who is in a book club, as I am, knows that when it's your turn to host, you find yourself scouring the pages of whatever you are reading to come up with an appropriate meal to make (or order) and beverage to serve. As far as I'm concerned, any book set anywhere near the Caribbean gives license to eat jerk chicken and drink rum.

Oddly, reading cookbooks often *satisfies* my hunger. If I look at one great recipe, my mouth starts watering. But by the time I've looked at a few dozen dishes, my confused mind is happy to settle for a cup of tea.

Also, like most cookbook fans, I tend to read them in bed after I've brushed my teeth and before I sleep. The great baking books inspire sweet dreams; the best international books transport me around the world; and the books of healthy cooking send me to sleep feeling virtuous just for having read them. But some cookbooks take my dreams much further: they inspire me not just to want to bake, travel, or eat more healthful food—but to live a better life. Some of the cookbooks I own and read are among the wisest books I've ever owned or read.

There's *Home Cooking: A Writer in the Kitchen*, by Laurie Colwin. This is a book from 1988 that people who love food and who love good writing tend to love. Colwin celebrates what she calls home food: meals like "a savory beef stew with olives and buttered noodles, a plain green salad with a wonderful dressing, and some runny cheese and chocolate mousse for dessert. Heaven!"

She writes, "We live in an age of convenience foods and household appliances. We do not have to slaughter pigs, pluck chickens, or make soap and candles. We do not hand-wash clothes. Machines often wash our dishes for us—and still everyone complains that they hardly have any time. The American family, we are told, is falling apart. It does not dine: it grazes from snack to snack."

Colwin admits that she has "no idea whether or not the American family is falling apart." But she does "know that many people still like to cook for their family, but that when they rush home after a day at the office they may not have a lot of time and energy to spend on cooking." What she provides is a book of essays about cooking and food and life. And she includes an important caveat up front: "These essays were written at a time when it was becoming increasingly clear that many of our fellow citizens are going hungry in the streets of our richest cities. It is impossible to write about food and not think about that."

These are elegant essays about topics from all the equipment you might ever need in the kitchen to how to disguise vegetables (from adults as well as from children) to feeding a crowd to easy cooking for exhausted people. And at the end of almost every essay is a simple and satisfying recipe: potato pancakes, shepherd's pie, old-fashioned steamed chocolate pudding, salt-free baked chicken with garlic and apples, and a black cake from the West Indies that is "to fruitcake what the Brahms piano quartets are to Muzak."

In one chapter, on what she calls nursery food, a specific category of home cooking that evokes the wonderful, mushy, fork-only meals of childhood, she writes of the comfort that old favorites can bring, and how she was filled with gratitude after a friend made her a shepherd's pie after the death of her father. It was just what she didn't know she wanted.

"Parts of a nursery dinner," she writes, "should be eaten without any utensils at all: corn sticks, cookies, steamed carrots and baby lamb chops." The ideal is "something comforting and savory, easy on the digestion—something that makes one feel, if even for only a minute, that one is safe. A four-star meal is the right thing when the human animal is well rested and feeling rich, but it is not much help to the sore in spirit who would be much better off with a big bowl of homemade soup."

Colwin was a novelist, short-story writer, and essayist; she died suddenly, of a heart attack, at age forty-eight in 1992. She left a husband, a daughter, eight works of fiction, and two beloved books about food and life, the second one a sequel to *Home Cooking* called *More Home Cooking*.

Nigella Lawson is another cookbook author who, in writing about the role that food plays in our lives, writes about life. And about death.

Nigella's sister, mother, and first husband all died of cancer. In her book *Feast: Food to Celebrate Life*, she ends with a chapter about food at funerals and what you can bring to those who are grieving.

"It may seem odd to talk about what you eat at a funeral as a way of celebrating life," she writes, "but at every level, that is exactly what it is. Nor do I mean a celebration in that cheery, if faintly maudlin sense of giving someone a good send-off, though that is a part of it. Any food is a vital reminder that life goes on, that living is important. That isn't brutal: it's the greatest respect you can pay to the dead."

Nigella describes how for some the act of eating "can seem like the cruelest demonstration of the dreadful disparity that now exists" between the living and the dead. But she reminds readers that you cannot bridge this gap "by acting as if you, too, have died."

She also wisely points out that no one is given a choice as to how they will react: "some eat out of grief, some lose their appetite." And she explains how food "marks a connection between the living. There is nothing you can say to someone who is bereaved that can make anything better and even the notion that you could make it better can feel offensive, even if the wish is declared out of kindness. But you can help, you can make food. And if you can't cook, or haven't got time, you can shop." The one thing she implores you not to do if you are shopping for someone who is grieving is to ask questions, like "what they'd like you to get or what they might want to eat. Decisions are impossible: you have to do it, and do it without drawing attention to the act."

As an example, Nigella describes how a friend left some bags of groceries for her on her doorstep when she was grieving. "She hadn't told me she was going, she hadn't asked what I needed: she just left the bags outside the side door with a short note." Nigella comments that it was "one of the kindest things anyone could have done."

The Taste of Country Cooking by Edna Lewis is a book filled with stories of generosity and kindness. It is as much a poetic memoir as it is a cookbook, and reading it brings me from my city apartment to a place I've never been: Freetown, Virginia, where Edna Lewis was born in 1916.

Lewis begins her book by telling the reader that Freetown was "a community of farming people. It wasn't really a town. The name was adopted because the first residents had all been freed from chattel slavery and they wanted to be known as a town of Free People." Her grandfather, she writes, was one of the founders.

The restaurateur and activist Alice Waters, in her foreword to the thirtieth-anniversary edition of *The Taste of Country Cooking*, writes this about Lewis and her classic book: "She enjoyed a childhood that could only be described as idyllic, in which the never-ending hard work of farming and cooking both sustained and entertained an entire community. In 1976, with the publication of this lovely, indispensable classic of a cookbook, she brought her lost paradise of Freetown back to life. Thanks to this book, a new generation was introduced to the glories of an American tradition worthy of comparison to the most evolved cuisines on earth, a tradition of simplicity and purity and sheer deliciousness that is only possible when food tastes like what it is, from a particular place, at a particular point in time."

Waters compares Lewis to "another notable advocate of simplicity, Mahatma Gandhi," who "famously remarked that we must become the change we want to make in the world.

Like Gandhi, Miss Lewis was as radical as she was traditional. To become the change she wanted to make, she left the racially divided South and plunged into the maelstrom of New York City, working variously as a typesetter for the *Daily Worker* and as a dressmaker for Marilyn Monroe, among other jobs, before she became the chef of an East Side restaurant in Manhattan called Café Nicholson and, later, of Gage & Tollner in Brooklyn."

Edna Lewis would go on to found the Society for the Revival and Preservation of Southern Food. She would be named Grande Dame des Dames d'Escoffier International. And she would write three other books, two alone, and one with her friend Scott Peacock. She died in Decatur, Georgia, in 2006, at the age of eighty-nine.

The Taste of Country Cooking is organized by season. Lewis walks the reader through all of the harvests and traditions and holidays, meal by meal. There's an Early Spring Dinner after Sheep-Shearing, and a Midsummer Sunday Breakfast, and a Morning-After-Hog-Butchering Breakfast, and a Dinner Celebrating the Last of the Barnyard Fowl. There are feasts: Emancipation Day and Christmas Dinners.

Just as each season has its meals, each meal has its recipes. My favorites are Lewis's citron preserves, new cabbage with scallions, hot buttered beets, braised leg of mutton, caramel layer cake, oyster stew, hickory nut cookies, beef kidney pie in puff pastry, smothered rabbit, dandelion wine, and her shad with roe. And the best recipe ever for eggs sunny-side up.

It's a book that ends with four of the sweetest words in the English language: "Serve with warm gingerbread."

So that's the food. But Lewis presents the ethos behind the food. She writes, "Whenever there were major tasks on the farm, work that had to be accomplished quickly (and timing is important to farming), then everyone pitched in, not just family but neighbors as well. And afterward we would all take part in the celebrations, sharing the rewards that follow hard labor. The year seemed to be broken up by great events such as hog butchering, Christmas, the cutting of ice in winter, springtime with its gathering of the first green vegetables and the stock going away to summer pasture, the dramatic moment of wheat threshing, the excitement of Revival Week, Race Day, and the observance of Emancipation Day. All of these events were shared by the whole community, young and old alike. I guess that is why I have always felt that the people of Freetown were very special. They showed such love and affection for us as children, at the same time asking something of us, and they knew how to help each other so that the land would thrive for all. Each family had its own different talents, its special humor, but they were bound together in an important way."

This is a book about looking after one another, and looking after the future: "If you have a spot of land, do plant a few apple trees, particularly if there are children around to enjoy them. We are still enjoying the apples from trees our parents planted 45 years ago."

Lewis describes her childhood with joy. She writes lovingly of her parents; and the excitement of having cousins come to visit; and the joy of going shoeless from March until the end of summer; and of making ice cream; and being too excited Christmas Eve to eat more than the oyster stew that began the feast.

Near the end of *The Taste of Country Cooking*, in the section on late-winter feasts, comes a passage that reminds the reader how precious and hard-won was this idyllic childhood:

> It was in between these daily chores that the people of Freetown found more time for visiting each other. There were visitors from nearby communities, especially to visit with Grandpa. A person of his age group (80 years and older) would arrive on horseback or in a buggy, unbridle his horse, and put it in the barn with ours. Then he would visit us for a week or two or three. We liked having visitors. It gave the house a festive air and neighbors would drop by to greet the guest. We children were able to be alone in the next room and relax our behavior without being noticed. A great fire would be going in the fireplace, and we would serve homemade cake and homemade wines that seemed to have been made for just such occasions. There would be lively conversations, with the aged men doing most of the talking and the young adults of my father's age group listening. I would be listening, too, hanging between my father's knees and watching the logs burning in the fireplace and bugs desperately trying to escape from the burning logs with only me being aware of their desperate plight. I was

too young then to understand why so much time was spent in discussion. It was only afterward that I realized they were still awed by the experience of chattel slavery fifty years ago, and of having become freedmen. It was something that they never tired of talking about. It gave birth to a song I often heard them sing, "My Soul Look Back and Wonder How I Got Over."

This world that Edna Lewis describes to us so lovingly, that inspires readers to want to celebrate the seasons and do more for our communities and plant trees that will bear fruit long after we are gone—this world, as she tells us at the beginning and end of her book, was created by people who grew up enslaved.

In a *New York Times Magazine* article about this book, food writer and cookbook editor Francis Lam writes about the foundational role that Edna Lewis and black southern cooking played in the creation of today's American cuisine. Lam also writes about the world in which Lewis grew up and lived: "She wrote *The Taste of Country Cooking*, in her 50s, in the 1970s, after years as a political radical, after the civil rights movement, after marching for the Scottsboro Boys." He quotes Lewis's friend Peacock saying, "She could see the ugly in the world." But, Lam adds, Lewis "refused to let the past, her past, be defined by anyone else but her."

A cookbook can do far more than give recipes for tasty dishes: it can introduce us to new places, help us celebrate life, comfort us in loss, and show us how to live. A cookbook can even remind us of America's original sin, which is manifest in the countless inequities that exist to this day, and inspire us to listen more carefully to one another and do more to fix our world. And it can help us remember to be grateful for the labor of those who farm and bring us the food we eat, and for the extraordinary gift of having meals every day and people we love to share them with.

"Bartleby, the Scrivener"
Quitting

BARTLEBY, a clerk in a story by Herman Melville, is the patron saint of quitters. He's the yin to the yang of Ahab, the Melville character who absolutely refuses to quit in his pursuit of Moby Dick, a big white whale.

I found myself thinking of Bartleby at a tech conference in Austin, Texas. I was listening to a lecture by a famous venture capitalist who had made hundreds of millions for his investors and himself by funding Internet start-ups. In his speech, he rattled off the names of some global business legends, people who had founded many of the world's most successful companies. He asked the audience to consider what these people had in common. Then he answered the question he had just posed:

"They never gave up."

I found this inspiring. It's not an original message. But it's a compelling one. We've been told this all our lives: Winners never quit, and quitters never win. But as I pondered it more that day, it began to gnaw at me. First, all these business legends probably *had* quit something—school or another career. Maybe they'd originally wanted to be jazz musicians and basketball stars, and maybe they quit those pursuits. That they didn't quit the activity that finally made them famous tells me very little. And is obvious.

That's when Bartleby popped into my head.

I parked that thought.

Then I came across a video that was being widely shared on the Internet. It was a graduation speech at the University of Texas at Austin given by a genuine hero, a man who had for thirty-seven years served the United States with great honor as a Navy SEAL and who had attained the rank of admiral and commander of US Special Operations. He was giving advice on how to change the world, based on his experiences from navy training, the SEALs being the elite special forces arm of the US Navy. It seemed to me to be excellent advice—starting with making your bed every morning, something my mother also taught me (though it didn't quite stick). But then came the end of the speech. He was describing a bell that was in the center of the training compound. And he said that when you rang the bell during SEAL training, it meant you were done, finished, you quit. The bell was always there. You could ring it at any time. You could ring it if the training was too grueling, if you no longer wanted to wake up at 5:00 a.m., if you were sick of swimming in freezing water, if you were worn out, if you decided that this whole Navy SEAL thing just wasn't for you.

His advice was simple, he said. "If you want to change the world, don't ever, ever ring the bell."

And I thought, *Hell, no.*

I mean, sometimes you have to ring the bell. Or admit that your business is tanking. Or just plain give up. Even if you really want to change the world.

It's of course true that everyone who succeeds didn't give up—how could it be otherwise? But it's also true that many people kept going years after they should have stopped. Many people bankrupted themselves and their families pursuing a dream they had no chance of achieving. And in a culture where no one is allowed to fail, it's preferable to lie about where you are than admit you are in trouble, especially if that admission means that every lifeline will be immediately removed.

"Fake it till you make it" is great in theory. But often it really means fake it until you go under.

And as for not ringing that bell—that just doesn't make sense. The bell is there to be rung. If you realize that you don't have the stamina or motivation to be a Navy SEAL, then of course you should ring the bell. With no shame whatsoever. The last thing we want in the Navy SEALs are people who don't think they have what it takes to be there. And they should be encouraged to self-identify as soon as possible.

Bartleby popped back into my head.

I'm a longtime bell ringer. I bail. If I'm reading a book and I don't care for it, I stop. At the theater, if I'm bored, I'll leave. I will wait until intermission—but then I'll run, not walk, to the nearest exit.

The other day I was watching a television show and saw footage of a young British man who decided he really wanted to try bungee jumping—the extreme sport where you plunge off a bridge or tower and hurtle toward the ground, with the only thing coming between you and death (or horrid injury) a rubber cord fixed around your ankles. This young man got to the top of a bungee platform in Thailand and was all set to jump. He confessed at that moment to being more than a little scared. Not uncommon in the world of bungee—the woman who was set to jump right before him had decided, after several minutes of hesitation, not to jump. Back down she went.

Again, there was Bartleby.

But this fellow decided to ignore his fear. So he jumped anyway. And something happened that almost never happens: the cord became detached from his ankles. And so he didn't bounce right back up as he expected but rather plunged like a missile into the hard surface of a lake. He was going eighty miles per hour when he hit the water, and he sustained grievous injuries. His spleen ruptured on impact; his liver tore; his lungs collapsed. He almost died. Only after a month in the hospital in Bangkok was he able to return home.

That's what *can* happen if you don't quit when the voice in your head tells you to. But there's also a danger to quitting every time you experience fear or uncertainty or anxiety or trepidation. If you do that, you miss out on adventure and excitement. You don't expand your world. And sometimes no matter how much you might like to quit, you really shouldn't.

The key is knowing what's at stake.

Certainly a great deal was at stake when Winston Churchill said in a 1941 speech, "Never give in, never give in, never, never, never, never—in nothing, great or small, large or petty—never give in except to convictions of honor and good sense."

Thank goodness Winston Churchill and the British people had such firm resolve during World War II. Ringing the bell, as it were, would have been catastrophic for the world. Sometimes quitting isn't an option. But much of the time, it is.

Often, though, the hardest thing isn't quitting—it's staying quit. People may try to coax you back into the game. You may well try to do that to yourself.

It can be very hard to stick to giving up, much harder than persevering. The reason for persevering is often clear—as it was for the British and Churchill in 1941. And sometimes it's clear on a much more modest scale—I'm not giving up because I don't want to and I don't have to. That's as good a reason as any.

But the reasons for calling it a day (and keeping it called) are frequently less obvious. Perhaps it's plain old fear, as experienced by our first prospective bungee jumper. Or boredom and irritation, as it so often is when I put down a book or leave a show. The world demands an answer. Often we don't have one.

Literature gives remarkably little guidance to those of us who constantly grapple with the urge to quit—but we do have Bartleby the Scrivener in the short story of the same name, which Melville published two years after *Moby-Dick*. (The subtitle is "A Story of Wall Street.")

Bartleby's tale is told by the head of a law office who has two clerks (law copyists, also known as scriveners) and an office boy working for him. He brings in a third clerk, the enigmatic Bartleby, "pallidly neat, pitiably respectable, incurably forlorn."

As our narrator describes, "At first Bartleby did an extraordinary quantity of writing. As if long famishing for something to copy, he seemed to gorge himself on my documents. There was no pause for digestion. He ran a day and night line, copying by sun-light and by candle-light. I should have been quite delighted with his application, had he been cheerfully industrious. But he wrote on silently, palely, mechanically."

Bartleby works quietly and steadily for two days until he is asked, on the third, to perform a routine task: his boss needs help comparing a brief document with its copy. "Imagine my surprise, nay, my consternation," the narrator writes, "when without moving from his privacy, Bartleby in a singularly mild, firm voice, replied, 'I would prefer not to.'"

That's just the start of Bartleby's insubordination. Bartleby refuses more and more tasks, again with that phrase, though he does continue diligently copying documents. Other odd behaviors emerge; it seems Bartleby is living at the office. Eventually, after attempting to reason with Bartleby, our narrator gives up and decides he must fire Bartleby, albeit with generous severance. But he is unsuccessful in that: Bartleby would prefer not to leave. Our narrator then moves the office to another building to rid himself of Bartleby. But even this doesn't work: Bartleby refuses to leave even when the old office has new tenants. And always with that phrase, "I would prefer not to." Finally, after Bartleby has defied all entreaties to vacate the premises, the police are called, and he is hauled off to prison, where he prefers not to sustain his own life.

What makes Bartleby so radical is not that he refuses to do what's asked of him; it's that he refuses to give a reason. He refuses to tell the narrator a single thing about himself, not where he was born, not anything. He even refuses to give a reason why he won't say anything. Bartleby has quit explaining himself solely because he prefers not to. And this is the most irksome and revolutionary act imaginable. As our infuriated narrator observes: "Nothing so aggravates an earnest person as a passive resistance."

Sure, Henry David Thoreau quit the world of possessions to retire to a cabin in the woods—but he then wrote a whole book, *Walden*, explaining why and what he found. That's the model. If you quit your job, you are likely to have an exit interview. Sure, you are free to answer, "I would prefer not to." But most people bow to the pressure and wind up explaining themselves. If I quit Facebook for even a few days, I feel as though I owe the world an explanation and usually give one.

There's a noble history of resigning in protest. Everyone understands that—the noisy, principled exit, where you announce the reason that you can no longer participate or even bear to have your presence count as an endorsement. But just plain quitting? That frays the fabric of society.

There are some things that I probably quit too early. I would love to play the piano, but I couldn't be bothered to practice and soon gave it up. And there are things that I probably should have quit far earlier than I did. I've made some terrible business decisions in my time and have been guilty of pouring good company money after bad because I was too stubborn to admit even to myself that I had made a mistake.

Admittedly, Bartleby may not be the most appealing model of resistance, and yet the purity of his stance, and the confidence with which he manages to maintain it, offer a weirdly refreshing touchstone in a society that is terrified of people who can't be threatened or induced to participate in activities they don't like. I don't worry that the world will ever suffer from a lack of piano players or people like me to applaud them. But I do worry that we don't offer one another enough support when we just want to quit what we are doing for no reason other than that we would prefer not.

The Gifts of the Body
Losing

WHEN A WRITER DIES, all the books she or he might have written die, too.

I first heard about AIDS in an article in the *New York Times* on July 3, 1981. I was soon to be nineteen and had just finished my freshman year of college. The headline was "Rare Cancer Seen in 41 Homosexuals." Scary. But not too scary. I mean, after all, it was only forty-one.

So I didn't give it much thought. The next year, I took a break from college. I went to Los Angeles in what would have been my fall term junior year to make my fame and fortune in television. I found work as a temporary secretary, a substitute English teacher, and a production assistant for a television show; then I landed a job as personal assistant to a director. He needed someone who could type and drive. My driving isn't nearly as good as my typing. In fact, it's terrible. But he didn't seem to mind.

I was twenty, living on my own in Los Angeles, and I

went a little wild. I had a boisterous group of pals, and we would meet nightly at a bar called Motherlode before heading off to dance at Studio One (which had the motto "For the Eighties"). To the intoxicating beat of "Muscles" sung by Diana Ross and "Searchin'" by Hazell Dean and "State of Independence" by Donna Summer and "Mickey" by Toni Basil and "Maneater" by Hall and Oates, we would gather, dance, gossip. It was a motley crew: a larcenous kept boy with shoulder-length blond hair; a gorgeous dancer I adored (he is still one of my favorite people), who could hold a pencil between his pecs; the dancer's volatile roommate, who had a wickedly caustic sense of humor—these were a few of the gang. We had endless time for one another and never seemed to have to buy a drink: they simply appeared. In our crew there was also a blandly handsome fellow named Edward. Edward and I weren't particularly drawn to one another, but if the lights came up and there was no one else left around we might just go home together. Or at least we did five or six times, and wound up doing just about everything two guys could think of to do.

Then Edward stopped showing up night after night at Motherlode, and eventually I called him. He felt terribly ill, he told me, but he wasn't sure what was going on: he kept losing weight; his glands were swollen; he woke up in the middle of the night drenched in sweat. He was a little scared, if only because no one could figure out what was wrong with him.

I offered to take him out for a meal if he was up for it, and we went to IHOP, the International House of Pancakes.

I made him eat their chocolate-chip pancakes—to put some weight on him, and also because they are so delicious. That was the last time I saw Edward. He moved back to Hawaii.

During and right after our IHOP meal, I didn't give Edward's illness much thought. He could have had a flu or a stomach bug or any one of a million ailments from which one soon recovers. But later word came that he had died, and no one knew why. It was all very strange, but none of us had been that close to him.

When I returned to college in spring 1983, I reconnected with my parents' friend, and by then mine, the writer Larry Kramer. He was devoting all his time to a group he'd cofounded, Gay Men's Health Crisis. More and more people were dying of what was first called GRID—gay-related immune deficiency. Talking with Larry scared the hell out of me. Especially when I realized that Edward had almost certainly died of what is now called AIDS.

Larry convinced me that this disease that was affecting hundreds of people would soon affect thousands and then millions. But no one was doing or saying a thing about it. A Tylenol poisoning that killed seven people had been front-page news day after day; so had an outbreak of Legionnaires' Disease a few years before that had killed twenty-nine people. But here was a disease affecting gay men, for the most part, and because of that no one seemed to care.

When eventually AIDS did start to get press, the result was hysteria. Fifteen percent of the country thought people who had AIDS should be tattooed to identify them; more than half the country thought everyone with AIDS should be quarantined. The atmosphere was more horrible than it is possible to describe. Hospitals turned away dying people at their doors. Those lucky enough to be in a hospital often weren't brought food—it was left outside the room door. People with visible lesions were shunned in the streets and turned away from businesses. So were people who just "looked" or "acted" gay.

The disease subsumed my last two college years. I staged fund-raisers and volunteered for the newly formed AIDS Project New Haven, leaving the campus one or two evenings a week to work as a volunteer on their hotline. It was challenging to reassure callers when there was no reassuring information to share. I certainly didn't feel reassured. In my head, I did the math. Everyone who had this disease was dying. There was Edward. He was dead. There were so many others that I'd been with, in Los Angeles and before. (Even before "officially" coming out at age eighteen, I had been making up for lost time.) And so many of them were sick.

I figured it was likely I wouldn't see thirty, or even twenty-five. And there was also the dread-filled thought that perhaps I had unwittingly condemned others to the same fate, a fear that was so intense that I shared it only once, with David Baer, and never mentioned it again to anyone. David was one of the few people in whom I could confide; he had the same fears.

Being at college during this period was surreal: my days were spent in dining halls and classes with people whose biggest care in the world appeared to be whether they would or wouldn't pass a certain test or get a paper in on time or land a part in a play; many of my evenings and weekends were spent talking with young men who were dying.

Volunteering was how I staved off panic.

So I also volunteered for Gay Men's Health Crisis (now referred to mostly as GMHC) when in New York on vacations—occasionally as a buddy bringing groceries to those homebound, but mostly on the hotline. The hotline was run from a tiny room in a brownstone building in the Chelsea neighborhood of Manhattan. I had a routine: work as a temporary secretary during the day; then buy a burrito from a shop called Kitchen in Chelsea; then scarf down bites of it as I sat for hours answering call after call after call.

My supervisor at GMHC was named Barry. He was tall, gangly, mostly bald, and had an acid tongue. That was all I knew about him; Barry wasn't one for small talk. Or at least not with me.

Night after night, I fielded awful calls. And what made it more awful was that we still had so little information and so few resources. There was often almost nothing we could do other than listen.

Then, one night, I reached my limit. I had talked to a young man who was sitting at home with the corpse of his lover and couldn't get a single funeral home in the city to take the body away. I'd helped him dial his way through our list until finally we found one. Another call was from a guy who was in NYC illegally and wanted to know if he could be deported for being sick. He was sobbing. Or maybe he was having trouble breathing from PCP pneumonia. I could barely hear him. I kept having to say "Excuse me" and "Could you repeat that?" We had a lawyer who might have been able to help him, but I couldn't get the guy on the phone to trust me enough to leave any information or visit during the day. Another call was from an older man, gay but not out of the closet, whose glands were swollen and who was having terrible night sweats. Was it AIDS? This was still years before there was any kind of test, before anyone knew what caused it, before anyone really knew what it was. All I could tell him to do was to see a doctor. I had one I could recommend.

The phone rang just as I was getting ready to head out.

"GMHC Hotline, can I help you," I said.

The voice on the other end of the phone belonged to a young woman.

"How do you know if you have AIDS?" she asked.

"Well," I answered. "There's no test, but it's diagnosed when you have one of the opportunistic infections associated with it. There are some symptoms that many people have, though. Night sweats, swollen glands that have been swollen and stay swollen for several weeks, weight loss. But those could be other things, too. In fact, if you check your glands too often, you'll make them swell. They aren't made to be constantly prodded."

There was silence on the phone.

"Do you have any of those?" I asked.

"No," the young woman said.

"Any other physical symptoms. Lesions? Anything?" I then was sure to add, "You know I'm not a doctor. So I can't diagnose anything, and even if I was, I couldn't do it on the phone. If you're worried, you should really just go see your doctor. If you don't have a doctor, I can give you the name of one."

"Okay," she said. "But how do you get it?"

"Well, we don't really know. But it seems to be sexually transmitted. It also seems to be passed among IV drug users sharing needles." As trained, I didn't press.

"Well, I'm scared that I got it. You see, I think my hairdresser is gay."

Suddenly, I had a sense where this call might be headed.

"Okay," I said. "That wouldn't be unusual. There are a lot of gay hairdressers."

"Yeah," she repeated. "I'm pretty sure he's gay. And I just came back from the salon. And he washed my hair. And now I'm thinking that he might have given me AIDS. You know. He had his hands in my hair."

"Oh my God," I said, unable to keep that to myself. I then went way off script. "Look, I have to ask you a question."

"Okay," she said.

"Do you have a pen and paper nearby? And a small suitcase?"

"Yes," she said.

Barry seemed to appear from nowhere. I don't know how he knew what I was going to say next, but he grabbed the phone from my hand and calmly reassured the young woman. After he was done, he turned back to me.

"And why, might I ask, even though I think I know, were

you asking that caller if she had a pen and paper and a small suitcase?"

I fessed up. I was about to tell her to write a note to her family saying goodbye, scribble a quick final will and testament, and then pack some small items in the suitcase and go right to the nearest emergency room to spend the short time on earth she had left.

"That's exactly what I feared. Maybe you need a night off."

"But really, Barry! From her hairdresser? Because he might be gay? What an idiot! What a hateful idiot!"

I was furious. At her. And at Barry.

"Take your burrito, and get the hell out of here. I'll see you tomorrow. Less hysterical and more compassionate, please." As I closed the door, I think I heard Barry laugh. But he never admitted to me that he thought it was funny.

For decades, I tried not to think too much about that time, mostly because I couldn't. It's as though it all happened to someone else, somewhere else. I couldn't remember how I felt. I remember the common phrase people would share, that it was like some of us were at war, and we were surrounded— at work, on the subway—by people who were at peace. Even though I was in my twenties, I just got used to the fact that friends got sick and died: after Edward, there was Hugh and Stan and John and Jim and Craig and so many more. It didn't stop being sad, horrible, terrifying. But it stopped being weird. It just was.

One book I read recently brought it all back: *The Gifts of the Body* by Rebecca Brown, the sixth book by a writer who has gone on to write six more; her work includes essays, a memoir about her mother's death, plays, and story collections.

The Gifts of the Body is a slender novel in eleven connected stories, narrated by a home-care worker as she describes her visits to various people with AIDS. Each chapter is named for a different "gift"—the gifts of sweat, wholeness, tears, skin, hunger, mobility, death (yes, death), speech, sight, hope, and mourning. Perhaps the author had been reading Anne Morrow Lindbergh's *Gift from the Sea* when she decided on this structure. And there is something similar in tone: both are quiet and thoughtful books.

But the subject matter is totally different. *The Gifts of the Body* is a book that captures not just the horrors of the early years of the AIDS plague but also the toil, drudgery, mundanity of it all. There are stories here of women with AIDS, though most of the people the narrator visits are gay men.

Brown was a home-care worker. I know this only from her bio on the back of the book, but I think I would have been able to guess it regardless. The observations throughout the book aren't just convincing—they have the immediacy of entries in a diary.

"I cleaned the bathroom," she wrote. "I shook cleanser in the shower and sink and cleaned them. I sprayed Windex on the mirror. When I was wiping it off I saw myself. My face was splotched. My t-shirt had a dark spot. I put my hands to it and sniffed them. They smelled like me, but also him. It was Rick's sweat. I put my hands up to my face and I could smell him in my hands. I put my face in my hands and closed my eyes. I stood there like that a while then I went to the kitchen."

She also wrote: "He wasn't getting any better. He was just getting worse more slowly."

And: "His sores were dark purple and about the size of quarters. The edges of them were yellow and his skin was dark brown. The sores weren't running or oozing or scabs because they always had this salve on them . . . I changed gloves several times when I was doing the salve because my gloves got coated with it, and also with his hair, which was very tight and curly and fell out easily, and with flecks or patches of skin. I think he felt embarrassed to have it done except it would have been worse not to have it done."

The Gifts of the Body reveals much about the lives of home-care workers. The author describes the paperwork, the scheduling, and the team meetings where they share their stories of their clients and their work, and seek help and advice and, sometimes, comfort from one another. But it's the clients who are most vivid, along with their friends, lovers, former lovers, and occasionally relatives who look after them. We learn about their jobs, their pets, the foods they like, their travels.

Two stories are about a man named Ed. In the first, "The Gift of Tears," Ed finally gets a coveted place in a hospice. But he's not ready. He explodes with rage, lashing out at the narrator, and then he is overwhelmed by grief but unable to cry, because something is wrong with his tear ducts. In the second, "The Gift of Mobility," the narrator goes to visit Ed at the hospice; she describes hugging him goodbye as usual:

When I was about to take my arms away he squeezed me tighter.

"I'm sorry I haven't been very nice lately," he said into my hair.

"Ed, you've been fine," I said. But I knew what he meant.

He was holding me, so I couldn't see his face. "I don't like being here anymore," he said. "I wish I could go away."

"I'm sorry, Ed," I said. My cheek was against his chest. I could feel his ribs.

"Everybody here dies," he said.

I squeezed him. I could hear his pulse, his heart. It sounded so normal.

"Remember when the guys used to think Super Ed would beat the system?"

I nodded. "Yeah."

He squeezed me and took a deep breath. His lungs sounded normal too. "All the guys who named me Super Ed are dead."

The Gifts of the Body was published in 1994. Rebecca Brown was writing in the midst of those many years—more than a decade—between when the plague was first reported and when finally, miraculously, thanks entirely to activism, medicines were discovered that can now keep it at bay. She writes about how, initially, everyone thought there would be a quick cure, and then how everyone came to believe it would never be cured. (I should note: there is still no cure.) About how people died quickly at first and then managed to live a year or two with the treatments at hand, but everyone still died: "After they died you missed them. But also there was a way you missed them before they died because you knew they were going to die."

She continues, "It took the epidemic going on for many years before there were any hospices. First there was one, then another. People could only go there when they had less than six months left to live. The idea was to have somewhere 'comfortable' to die. When the hospices opened there was a huge waiting list for the rooms, so you were lucky if you got one. But there was a quick turnover because everyone died so quickly. But the waiting list kept growing because more people got sick."

The Gifts of the Body did what my memory couldn't or wouldn't. It reminded me how I felt during that time. And maybe even taught me something about the smart-ass twenty-year-old answering phones in a little office in a brownstone in Chelsea, who was often too scared to think or feel.

When I do think back on those times, I try to remember all the people I knew who died. Every single one I can. That's what matters. Sure, *how* they died matters; *why* they died matters; *how many* died matters. That all matters, desperately, terribly. But *who* died matters more than anything else.

I think about my friends. I think about people I admired. And I often think about the writers. The world lost brilliant writers to AIDS: Paul Monette, Melvin Dixon, Robert Ferro, Michael Grumley, Assotto Saint, Stan Leventhal, Essex Hemphill, Vito Russo, Joseph Beam, Bruce Chatwin, John Boswell, Arturo Islas, Randy Shilts, and John Preston, to name a few. And then there were the readers. The world lost to AIDS hundreds of thousands of readers, who would have read and discovered and debated and been changed by these and so many other writers.

In Berlin there's a monument in Bebelplatz to make sure we never forget the May 1933 book burning by the Nazis. You can easily miss this monument—it's simply a glass square set among the cobblestones. When you stand on the glass, you look down into a cavernous white library—a library that is totally empty. Set deep into the square below the glass paver on which you stand is row after row of empty white shelving, enough shelf space to store all of the twenty thousand books that were burned there: books by Albert Einstein and Rosa Luxemburg and Erich Maria Remarque.

We can read the books that were written, books like *The Gifts of the Body*, and remember. But we can also remember the books that will never be written. And the readers who will never be there to read them.

The Little Prince
Finding Friends

I MET Antoine de Saint-Exupéry's little prince when I was eleven or twelve; as a preteen I found the book and its title character cloying. *The Little Prince* didn't charm me, and the little prince didn't either. There was all that talk of the difference between adults and children; there was the drawing that looked like a hat but was actually an elephant inside a snake; there was a journey from a small planet and the characters the little prince encountered along the way: a king, a geographer, and a businessman, to name a few. There was a flower and a sheep and a fox and a snake. And there was our narrator, about whom we knew very little, only that he was a pilot whose plane had gone down in the desert, and who had a limited amount of time—eight days, in fact—to fix the engine before he would perish of thirst.

Our narrator tells us the story of a little prince he meets in the desert. We learn that the prince is a visitor from another planet and that he has left a special flower there; he soon becomes terribly worried that a sheep might eat the flower.

Some people I knew—friends, and also adults—loved this little book. I remember seeing several people (once, two in a day) with tattoos of the iconic drawing of the little prince inked on some part of their body, even in the days long before everyone had a tattoo. A few also had a quote from the book etched on their skin: "One sees clearly only with the heart." The book's author had a tragic end that added another dimension to the story: Antoine de Saint-Exupéry was an acclaimed author and daring French flier who disappeared during a World War II reconnaissance mission. His plane went down somewhere in the Mediterranean as he was on his way from Corsica to Nazi-occupied France. This was one year and a few months after the publication of *The Little Prince*.

Having read the book as a preteen, I felt no need to read it again. I just assigned it to that enormous shelf of slender books that speak volumes to others but not to me.

I believe that we store memories in our muscles and our tendons and our bones, and they can remain hidden there for years. I'll bang my elbow at the dinner table and suddenly remember something from decades before, often something painful: a day I disappointed someone or was disappointed, or a time when I lost my temper and was ashamed of myself for it, or when someone yelled at me. It's not usually the happy memories I keep locked up in my body; it's the painful ones.

On an icy winter day last year, I was feeling restless and decided to walk to a local bookstore. I stepped off a curb and nearly tripped over a soda can lying in the gutter. As I felt a sharp twinge in my ankle, I suddenly found myself remembering Lee Harkins, a ninth-grade classmate who died of Hodgkin's lymphoma in the spring of our tenth-grade year. It had been years since I had thought of Lee, and that itself caused pain.

That same cold day, I bought *The Little Prince*, in the Richard Howard translation. I'm not sure why. It was on the front table of the local bookstore, Three Lives and Company, and I felt compelled to buy it. As I left the bookstore, it began to rain the kind of freezing rain that penetrates even the thickest garments, with a horizontal gusty wind that explodes umbrellas. So I went to a coffee shop to wait out the weather and started to read *The Little Prince*. And the more I read, the more I thought of Lee. There was no apparent connection. That's just how it happened.

Books can attach themselves to memories in unexpected ways. All at once, Lee's story and the story of the little prince started to merge in my mind.

Lee had long straight hair, caramel brown—not curly blond hair, as the little prince did. But there was something little prince–like about her: something curious, and open, and raw, and kind. She wasn't one of my closer friends that one term we went to school together—I didn't really know her very well at all—but she was a friend. My guess is that many of the eighty or so kids in our class thought of Lee as a friend. She wasn't sick when school began—or, rather, she was, but didn't know she was. She was just another kid, an awkward, shy, funny, clumsy, but athletic kid. A popular kid. People liked to be around her.

We were at boarding school, so it was an intense year— our first away from home. That may have been part of the reason we formed bonds with one another so quickly. Sometimes it was *Lord of the Flies*, but mostly not. We became a loose-knit family, living together twenty-four hours a day, seven days a week. We came in as little angels, most of us, and quickly started to push boundaries. There was no line between the kids who followed rules and those who didn't. It was still the 1970s, after all.

Then we went away for Christmas break. Then we came back. And then we heard Lee wasn't coming back. Her two best friends kept in close touch with her and visited her at home and in the hospital. And then she was gone, during our tenth-grade year. We raised some money for an organization she had started while she was sick, to help people who didn't have the kind of support she did while undergoing treatment for cancer. We dedicated our yearbook to her. We went to college. Some of us, myself included, sporadically kept in touch with Lee's mother. And then I didn't.

When our narrator in *The Little Prince*, our aviator shot down in the desert, begins to talk to us, he tells us that if he tries to describe the little prince, "it's so I won't forget him. It's sad to forget a friend. Not everyone has had a friend."

Lee died thirty-nine years ago. And the little prince, who

at the end of the book leaves our aviator and our planet, left many years before that. But if the little prince still exists whenever you look up at the night sky and ponder whether there's a flower somewhere out there that may or may not have been eaten by a sheep, why can't Lee still be present, too? Is she any more gone from my life than the dozens of classmates with whom I was also friends, but now haven't seen in thirty-nine years? Sure, they are alive. But are they any more alive to me? Perhaps they are less so.

In his travels on earth, the little prince comes upon a fox who has a simple request: he wants the little prince to tame him.

"I'd like to," the little prince replied, "but I haven't much time. I have friends to find and so many things to learn."

"The only things you learn are the things you tame," said the fox. "People haven't time to learn anything. They buy things ready-made in stores. But since there are no stores where you can buy friends, people no longer have friends. If you want a friend, tame me!"

"What do I have to do?" asked the little prince.

"You have to be very patient," the fox answered. "First you'll sit down a little ways away from me, over there, in the grass. I'll watch you out of the corner of my eye, and you won't say anything. Language is the source of misunderstandings. But day by day, you'll be able to sit a little closer. . . ."

And so the little prince tames the fox, and they become friends.

Lee was *our* friend. And, for most of us, fourteen-year-olds unaccustomed to death, she was the first friend we lost.

I thought about all of this as I sat there in that coffee shop, waiting for the freezing rain to stop. And I looked around me and saw, as I always do these days in coffee shops, a sea of laptops. Everyone together and alone in public. Next to me was a young couple, clearly on a date. I overheard snippets of nervous conversation. It was sweet—the girl had long, straight hair that kept falling in front of her face, at one point catching the froth of her cappuccino, like a boat flying through the crest of a frothy wave. The boy had a tattoo of a dagger on his neck. After a few awkward moments, he pulled out his mobile phone. To snap a picture or send a text. And then she did the same. And there they were, across from each other, on a date, in a Greenwich Village coffee shop, staring at their little screens. Every now and then one would show the other something. But most of the time they didn't; they just stared into the screens in their hands.

At one point in *The Little Prince*, after he meets the fox, the prince encounters a salesclerk who sells thirst-quenching pills: "Swallow one a week and you no longer feel any need to drink." The little prince asks the salesclerk:

"Why do you sell these pills?"

"They save so much time," the salesclerk said. "Experts

have calculated that you can save fifty-three minutes a week."

"And what do you do with those fifty-three minutes?"

"Whatever you like."

"If I had fifty-three minutes to spend as I liked," the little prince said to himself, "I'd walk very slowly toward a water fountain. . . ."

I grew up in a world without cash machines, where you had to know the people at the liquor store, because if they remembered you, you could count on them to cash a personal check when the bank was closed. Making reservations for flights or hotels or restaurants required phone calls. If the line was busy or unanswered, you needed to call back. There were no answering machines. Everything took longer.

It's not that I pine for the inconvenience of those days, but I do wonder what happens to the time. I should have so much more time. But I don't. And I don't know what I do with the time I have. I certainly don't use my extra fifty-three minutes a day to walk slowly toward a water fountain.

I do know that I waste a lot of time comparing water fountains. Nothing is good enough. The friend we are with isn't nearly as interesting as the friend who just texted us from across town. The restaurant we are in is fine, until we go on Yelp and see that there are dozens rated higher. Our smartphones bring us the world and tell us that something better, more fun, more exciting, more authentic, more hip, more moving is going on somewhere else.

I find myself returning again and again to one conversation, between the little prince and our narrator:

"People where you live," the little prince said, "grow five thousand roses in one garden . . . yet they don't find what they're looking for . . ."

"They don't find it," I answered.

"And yet what they're looking for could be found in a single rose, or a little water . . ."

"Of course," I answered.

And the little prince added, "But eyes are blind. You have to look with the heart."

When the little prince is getting ready to leave earth and his body and return to the place from whence he came, he says: "It's good to have had a friend, even if you're going to die. Myself, I'm very glad to have had a fox for a friend."

After I finished reading *The Little Prince* that day, I sat in the coffee shop for a while, until the freezing rain stopped for good, and then I started to walk home, but didn't. I walked all around the city. I was careful not to twist my ankle, and careful not to walk too fast. Off came the earbuds, piping into my head the random sound track to my life. Instead, I tried to look and hear. And I tried to remember every single thing I could about Lee.

What do we owe the dead, our dead? Maybe it's first that we need to remember them.

Lee lived at a time when photographs required film, which needed to be developed. The only picture I have of Lee is on the tribute page in our high-school yearbook. If it hadn't been for twisting my ankle, I might have gone years more without thinking of her again. Now, thanks to *The Little Prince*, I will always think of them together.

On Lee's tribute page, the dedication reads:

Love lives on.

The best of what we mortals are, and what we create, lives on.

In a spiritual sense. And in other ways, too.

Think how much poorer the world would be if, for instance, the words of Shakespeare or the music of Beethoven were silenced with their composer's passing. How fortunate we are that it doesn't happen that way.

Every time a school boy reads Hamlet's soliloquy . . . every time a young girl sits at the piano and begins to play the graceful notes of the Moonlight Sonata . . . a brilliant idea of a strong emotional feeling bursts to life once again.

Ideas live on. Gifts and talents live on. Acts of caring live on.

Love lives on.

Recently I got back in touch with Lee's mother, after more than thirty years.

Lee's mom is now retired from her executive director role running the ever-growing organization she and Lee founded, and also from a postretirement career as a hospital chaplain. And the name of that organization she and Lee created to help people undergoing treatment for cancer? It's called, quite simply, Lee's Friends.

1984
Disconnecting

IMAGINE IF there were a law decreeing that every citizen had to carry a tracking device and check it five times an hour. This device was to be kept at hand at all times. The law also decreed that you needed to place this device on your bedside table at night, so that it was never more than two feet away from your body, and if you happened to wake up in the middle of the night, then you needed to check it. You had to check it during mealtimes, at sporting events, while watching television. You even needed to sneak a quick peek at it during plays and weddings and funerals. For those unwilling to check their devices at the plays, weddings, and funerals, exceptions would be made—so long as you kept your device on right up until the moment the play, wedding, or funeral was beginning and then turned it on again the second the event was over, checking it as you walked down the aisle toward the exit.

Imagine, too, that whenever you went to a concert you

weren't allowed to view the actual concert but instead had to view it through your device, as though every concert were a solar eclipse and you would go blind if you stared at the thing itself. Only if you were holding your device in front of your face and viewing the event on its small screen would you be allowed to experience heightened moments of artistry and life.

Such a law would be deemed an insane Orwellian intrusion into our daily freedom, and people would rebel—especially when the law went even further. Imagine that the law decreed that it wasn't enough to check your machines; you needed to update the world on your activities on not one but several services, posting text, pictures, and links to let everyone know everywhere you went, and everything you ate, and everyone you saw. And when you weren't posting, the device would be tracking your movements and recording on distant servers where you were, whom you called, and what information you searched for.

Of course, these laws aren't necessary. We do this to ourselves.

So we now have to come up with elaborate ways to *stop* ourselves from engaging in this behavior. There are the restaurant dinners during which everyone puts their devices into the middle of the table, and the first person to reach for hers or his gets stuck with the bill for the whole crowd. There are programs you can buy that allow you to set a timer that keeps you from checking email or using apps or searching the Web for a certain period of time. One of these, in a truly Orwellian turn of phrase, is called Freedom. The thing that makes you free is the thing that constrains you.

It's easy to point to the damage caused by this culture we've created but perhaps more important to try to figure out why we are behaving this way.

Just a few weeks ago, I remember thinking with a slight bit of annoyance about a friendly acquaintance. He posts constantly to Facebook. At times you feel, if you follow him, that you are living his life alongside him. Usually, I enjoy his posts—he's smart and funny and accomplished, and writes with great style. He also has a lively group of friends, so you can count on his page to have interesting discussions. But this day, I was thinking: Enough. Enough of his friends, his dogs, his opinions.

Of course, no one was forcing me to read his posts—so I knew my irritation with him was irrational. But I was irritated. And clearly I wasn't the only person. Someone must have responded critically, because the next post was heartbreaking. It said something along the lines of this: "If you wonder why I post so often, it's because I'm lonely."

We check our smartphones constantly because we are lonely.

That's not the only reason, of course. But it's one.

We also check them too much because we are addicted to them, because we are impatient and they offer everything in an instant: from something to read to a listing of what's going on, to information about where to go, to a map to get us there. Checking them causes little bursts of pleasure hormones to fire in our brain—in anticipation of news, or something to laugh at, or something that will happily aggravate us, or the knowledge that our "friends" are "liking" and commenting on what we've done and shared.

We check them because we feel the need. Most people no longer work nine to five. If you work in an office, you are on call twenty-four hours a day, with emails popping up constantly that seem to require action, not to mention ever-newer forms of group communication through which your colleagues are constantly chiming in. And if you don't work in an office, you still need to be reachable at all times, too—perhaps because you are part of this new economy where we rent our time and talents and cars and homes and services to others in tiny increments.

We check them because we don't want to miss out. On anything.

I am not a Luddite. (As it turns out the Luddites weren't Luddites either—they weren't so much against the machinery as they were against losing their jobs, which is perfectly understandable.) I find my little device incredibly seductive. It makes my life easier in myriad ways and also provides a constant source of tunes. I need to remember very little—it's all there, my backup brain. I'm what a colleague used to call an early adapter, which is an early adopter who is perfectly willing to let the newest gadget show me how to run my life.

But I'm starting to believe that this is all madness and that we're already in way over our heads.

I can't help but think about my lonely Facebook friend,

and I fear that the very thing he is doing to stave off lone-liness may be exacerbating it. After each one of those tiny dopamine bursts comes a tiny dopamine hangover, a little bit of melancholy as the brain realizes that the thing we crave—to connect—hasn't really happened at all. It's like the feeling you get when you anticipate ordering something you love at a restaurant, and do so, and then are told that they just served the last one, and you will need to order something else. A little lift—they have lemon meringue pie—followed by a little fall: not for you. Our technology gives us the simu-lacrum of a connection but not the real thing.

George Orwell correctly predicted much about our world today.

In *1984*, Orwell describes how our hero Winston is sur-rounded everywhere by Big Brother and his slogans: WAR IS PEACE; FREEDOM IS SLAVERY; IGNORANCE IS STRENGTH. "He took a twenty-five cent piece out of his pocket. There, too, in tiny clear lettering, the same slogans were inscribed, and on the other face of the coin the head of Big Brother."

Winston lives in a world of constant surveillance but dares to keep a diary and to think for himself. Both crimes are punishable by death. Some of the monitoring is through tele-screens. Orwell writes, "He thought of the telescreen with its never-sleeping ear. They could spy upon you night and day, but if you kept your head you could still outwit them." Other monitors are the people around you. While sitting in his workplace cafeteria, Winston has "a pang of terror" when he notices a girl with dark hair looking at him. He's seen her before. "Why was she watching him? Why did she keep following him about?" He tries to remember if she was already at her table when he arrived and debates whether she's a member of the Thought Police or an amateur spy.

Orwell envisioned a world where all truth is what the government decides it is; where two plus two equals five, if that's the line; where lotteries keep the masses docile as each person waits for her or his chance to become rich. But he did not envision one where we spy endlessly on ourselves. And unlike most of us, Orwell's protagonist does everything in his power to escape the screens that surround him.

There's a portion of *1984* where Winston and the girl he loves do manage to escape the surveillance, or believe they do, and that's in a room above a secondhand shop in a "prole" part of town.

I first read *1984* in 1974. I was twelve, and the year 1984 seemed impossibly far in the future, as did the idea of ever being twenty-two years old. The novel fascinated me, even though I had no context for it. To me, it wasn't about fascism and had nothing to do with the Spanish Civil War or any class politics that I could figure out. It was just super creepy. Telescreens and pneumatic tubes bringing history that needed to be rewritten, thoughtcrimes and newspeak, and a secret Brotherhood plotting the overthrow of a ruling party that controlled everything—this was cool stuff. The only passages I didn't care for were the "lovey" ones, when Winston and Julia are together in their little room. I skimmed these.

Rereading the book as an adult, those were the passages that most captivated me. And one sentence in particular: "Winston became aware of silence, as one becomes aware of a new sound."

How often do I hear silence? Between the buds in my ears when I'm out and the screens that are on when I'm in, the answer is simple: hardly ever. I miss it. It's hard to remember what it sounds like and all the possibilities it allows.

Maybe that's the real tyranny of the smartphones and all the little screens everywhere. They help us rob ourselves of silence.

Epitaph of a Small Winner
Overcoming Boredom

IN SEVERAL OF its original Portuguese editions, *The Post-humous Memoirs of Bras Cubas* by Machado de Assis carries an evocative subtitle, which can be translated as *Epitaph of a Small Winner*. In the English translation I first read, this subtitle was adopted as the title. So that's what I call this remarkable novel, which is dedicated "To the first worm that gnawed my flesh." Thanks to reading the dedication, I knew right away that our narrator is dead. (Of course, had I read the book in Portuguese or in another English translation, the original title would have told me this; I also would have learned this fact had I first read the Susan Sontag foreword in my edition, as she rightly makes much of it.) The novel is divided into 160 very short chapters. And it begins with a disclaimer, in which our dead narrator lets us know that he doubts the book will be of interest to more than five or ten readers, tops.

Its author, Machado de Assis, lived and wrote in Brazil

in the nineteenth century, was the founder of the Brazilian Academy of Letters, and is one of the country's most revered writers. He also happened to be a favorite of Lin Yutang.

Sontag places *Epitaph of a Small Winner* "in that tradition of narrative buffoonery—the talkative first-person voice attempting to ingratiate itself with readers." She continues, "Ostensibly, this is the book of a life. Yet, despite the narrator's gift for social and psychological portraiture, it remains a tour of the inside of someone's head." She compares the book to one of Machado's favorites, *Journey Around My Room*, "a book by Xavier de Maistre, a French expatriate aristocrat (he lived most of his long life in Russia), who invented the literary micro-journey" when he was under house arrest for dueling. In de Maistre's highly experimental work, written in 1790, he describes traveling to various locations in his room: his walls, his chaise, his desk. More on that later.

Machado, born in Rio de Janeiro in 1839, was biracial. His father was a housepainter whose parents had been enslaved. His mother, a washerwoman for a rich family, was Portuguese by way of the Azores. Machado's mother died when he was nine. His father soon remarried, but then died a couple of years later.

Machado was mostly self-taught and was obsessed with literature from an early age. The translator into English for the edition I read, William L. Grossman, fills in some more details in his introduction to the volume, explaining that even though Machado published a large number of works in all different genres (including plays and poetry) before the age of forty, it wasn't until *Epitaph of a Small Winner* came out in 1880 that his reputation blossomed. Grossman adds that Machado worked as a government bureaucrat and that he married an aristocratic Portuguese woman who was five years older, and "who lived with him in what appears to have been complete harmony and devotion." They didn't have children. Machado's wife died in 1904; Machado in 1908, leaving more than a dozen works to be published posthumously.

Epitaph of a Small Winner is a book that, right from the start, meanders. The narrator halfheartedly apologizes for that: "The reader, like his fellows, doubtless prefers action to reflection, and doubtless he is wholly in the right. . . . However, I must advise him that this book is written leisurely, with the leisureliness of a man no longer troubled by the flight of time; that it is a work supinely philosophical, but of a philosophy wanting in uniformity, now austere, now playful, a thing that neither edifies nor destroys, neither inflames nor chills, and that is at once more than pastime and less than preachment."

Our dead narrator is named Bras Cubas. Hence the original title. He's every bit the maddening egotistical misanthrope that Sontag warned me (well, not just me but anyone who reads her foreword) that he would be. He's either constantly ill or a hypochondriac or both. He's pompous. Selfish. And his life is a series of blunders and disappointments and misunderstandings. He's convinced he's made a great discovery that will change the world, but nothing ever comes of it.

This is not a great man. But he's a modern one.

The book is filled with oddities. One chapter is nothing but a series of dots. It's titled "How I Did Not Become a Minister of State." Another chapter is titled "Unnecessary." It reads, in its entirety: "And, if I am not greatly mistaken, I have just written an utterly unnecessary chapter." It's unclear to me whether he's referring to the chapter at hand or the one before. I'm not sure it matters.

An early chapter is set in 1814, at the height of Napoleon's power. Our narrator's father hates the dictator; his uncle loves him. When news reaches Rio that Napoleon has fallen (fallen for the first time, our narrator hastens to point out), there is "great excitement" in the house. He writes of himself, then only nine years old:

> During those days, I cut an interesting figure wearing a little sword that my uncle had given me on St. Anthony's Day, and, frankly, the sword interested me more than Napoleon's downfall. This superior interest has never left me. I have never given up the thought that our little swords are always greater than Napoleon's big one. And please note that I heard many a speech when I was alive, I read many a page noisy with big ideas and bigger words, but (I do not know why), beneath all the cheers that they drew from my lips, there would sometimes echo this conceit drawn from my experience:
>
> "Do not deceive yourself, the only thing you really care about is your little sword."

Shortly after reading this passage, I decided to take a break from reading and found myself, as I so often do, checking Facebook, Twitter, Instagram, Pinterest, Hipstamatic, and, well, you get the point. And as I looked at all the posts, I was struck by the fact that, really, what everyone on social media was doing was sharing their little swords. And there I was, sharing mine. In a world of big books and big events and big ideas, of course there were some people commenting on these, and of course I was, too, sometimes. But mostly we were all reveling in the minutiae of our daily lives: our little meals, our little pets, our little observations, our little wry asides. As for those of us traveling, we were sharing our little delays and little discomfitures and little peeves: They had the wrong gate marked so I walked past it three times! The boarding was literally [actually, figuratively, as someone else pointed out, while going on to comment that frequent misuse of that word was a major pet peeve] a madhouse!

But maybe there is nothing wrong with that. Maybe that's what we've always done—on the village green, in the corridors of our apartment buildings, at breakfast with our families as we stood around the kitchen drinking coffee and spreading butter on English muffins. "How did you sleep?" is the first question we ask one another—not, "How did the president sleep?"

What has grown is our desire to share our little swords with absolute strangers. Sharing them with our friends and families is no longer enough. Increasingly, people want to make their little swords go viral, to get approval from the crowd, to have everyone acknowledge and proclaim that their little swords are as important as Napoleon's.

When I post something to social media, why do I do it? I really don't know. Part of it is the prompt—the various social-sharing programs are very good at encouraging you to add your voice to the chorus. One might ask you, "What's on your mind?" and so I answer. Another asks you to "Share," and so I do. Or maybe it lets you know that it's a friend's birthday and suggests that you write on her wall. Mostly, though, I'm not prompted: I want to add some encouragement or acknowledge a friend's joy or pain or simply reaffirm a social bond. Look at my little sword, my friend says. I like your little sword, I reply—meaning, I like you.

Then there's the shilling—for myself or for a friend: Visit this store! Buy this thing!

And then there's the type of post where someone advertises a contribution—literal or figurative—to a charity or cause. Boasting or helpful?

Our dead narrator in the Machado novel says of another character, "Naturally, he was not perfect. For example, after making a charitable contribution he always sent out a press release about it—a reprehensible or at least not praiseworthy practice, I agree. But he explained his conduct on the ground that good deeds, if made public, rouse people to do likewise—an argument to which one cannot deny a certain force."

People also like to share wisdom in the form of maxims on their social feeds, just as they always have in every medium.

Near the end of *Epitaph of a Small Winner* our dead narrator decides to "set down parenthetically a half dozen maxims." He describes them as "yawns born of boredom" but thinks "perhaps some aspiring essayist will find use for them as epigraphs."

They include:

One endures with patience the pain in the other fellow's stomach.

We kill time; time buries us.

A coach-man philosopher used to say that the desire to ride in carriages would be greatly diminished if everyone could afford to ride in carriages.

"Nothing could be more ridiculous than the childish delight that savages take in piercing a lip and adorning it with a piece of wood," said the jeweler.

I could share on social media any of these as my own tomorrow, and it would probably be enthusiastically received. As our narrator says, they were born of boredom. And people seeking a moment's escape from boredom would read them.

Of course, we know that the narrator is not just dead but fictional. *Epitaph of a Small Winner* is the work of one of the world's great writers, a master storyteller, who is treating us to a delightful, inventive, and absorbing novel that is all the more engaging thanks to its eccentric, bored, dyspeptic, infuriating narrator. There's something magical about this book. People say books made them laugh out loud; this one really did that to me. I underlined passages all the way through it. If this novel is the fruit of boredom, or an ode to it, bring it on.

Lin Yutang writes, "Perhaps all philosophy began with the sense of boredom. Anyway it is characteristic of humans to have a sad, vague and wistful longing for an ideal. Living in a real world, man has yet the capacity and tendency to dream of another world. Probably the difference between man and the monkeys is that the monkeys are merely bored, while man has boredom plus imagination."

So the question I find myself contemplating is what to do with my boredom. Should I distract it? That's what I do when I mindlessly scroll through news feeds or sit in front of the television cycling through channels, or pretend that flipping through a stack of magazines that has sat unread is a worthy project. Or should I engage it? That's when I question myself as to why I'm bored, though this often takes the form of a kind of self-flagellation, and winds up with my berating myself for not having planned some kind of activity: a trip to a museum or to the gym or to a movie. In those instances, boredom becomes something like jealousy, of others doing more worthwhile things or even of a version of myself who isn't so lazy and indolent.

In these moments of bored reflection, I don't create philosophy—what I create is a kind of accounting of my life.

Which is what the narrator of the Machado novel is doing from beyond the grave.

I've been trying increasingly to embrace and enjoy my boredom. In our distracted world, it's become a precious commodity. And of course, when I am no longer enjoying my boredom, the one sure cure is at hand: it's a book—the right book, or even just any decent book—that can instantly snap me out of it.

Zen in the Art of Archery
Mastering the Art of Reading

WHEN I MOST ENJOY READING, I'm not really conscious that I'm reading. It's at those moments when I'm so wrapped up in a book, so engrossed, so moved, so obsessed, or so fascinated, that the part of my mind that is watching me read—maybe keeping track of the pages or trying to decide how much longer I should keep on reading—that part of my mind has gone away.

This is what I hope for every time I open a book. It's something of a paradox. To love reading is to want to achieve the state where you don't know you are reading, where your communion with what you are reading is absolute. Or at least it is for me.

In my quest to understand this and maybe even be able to cultivate it, I went in search of books on reading. But most made me more aware, not less aware. They are like books on breathing—which cause me to think so much about my breathing I almost forget to breathe.

Then I found *Zen in the Art of Archery* by Eugen Herrigel.

Long before I read *Zen in the Art of Archery*, I read *Zen and the Art of Motorcycle Maintenance: An Inquiry into Values*, the 1974 classic by the philosopher Robert M. Pirsig, about a father and his son and their bike journey across half of the country. So I wrongly assumed that archery came after motorcycle, when in fact the opposite is true: the book on archery, published in 1948, was the inspiration for Pirsig's wonderfully odd title.

Zen in the Art of Archery is a small nonfiction book, originally written in German, and translated into English by R. F. C. Hull. If you give yourself an hour or two, you can start and finish it. But it's not a book that's going to reveal itself in an hour or two. In fact, it's a book that may well take me the rest of my life (and then some) to figure out.

The story is simple: Herrigel, a philosophy professor from Europe, is teaching in Japan and decides to learn the art of archery from a Japanese master. What he gets in addition to this is a lesson about Zen philosophy and about life.

He quickly realizes, "Bow and arrow are only a pretext for something that could just as well happen without them, only the way to a goal, not the goal itself, only helps for the last decisive leap."

In archery, the key skill is not aim—it's knowing how and when to let go of the arrow; how and when to let the arrow fly. Nothing else matters as much; nothing else is harder to get right.

Much of the book revolves around Herrigel's repeated attempts to master this one thing: letting go of the arrow.

But the heart of the book is Herrigel's struggle to become the kind of student he needs to be to learn from his teacher how to do this.

As he writes: "The Japanese pupil brings with him three things: good education, passionate love for his chosen art, and uncritical veneration of his teacher."

Herrigel is the opposite of this kind of pupil, at least at first. He's constantly questioning his teacher and trying to create his own systems and shortcuts.

"Archery is still a matter of life and death to the extent that it is a contest of the archer with himself; and this kind of contest is not a paltry substitute, but the foundation of all contests outwardly directed. . . ."

The problem with trying to figure out when to let the bowstring go is that it can't be figured out. You don't let the arrow fly, he learns; it's the arrow that does it. There is no you. There is only it.

When he questions the master on this, he's given the analogy of a child clutching the hand of a parent.

"You must hold the drawn bowstring," answered the Master, "like a little child holding the proffered finger. It grips it so firmly that one marvels at the strength of the tiny fist. And when it lets the finger go, there is not the slightest jerk. Do you know why? Because a child doesn't think: I will now let go of the finger in order to grasp this other thing. Completely unself-consciously, without purpose, it turns from one to the other. . . ."

The master also describes a bamboo leaf in winter that bends slowly from the weight of snow until the snow falls and the bamboo leaf springs back to where it was before it was weighted down. The snow doesn't decide to part from the leaf and the leaf doesn't decide that it's time to dump the snow. It just happens.

" 'The right art,' cried the Master, 'is purposeless, aimless.' "

Eventually, Herrigel does manage to get it right and, even later, to hit the target. But when he congratulates himself, his master has one more admonition: " 'You know already that you should not grieve over bad shots; learn now not to rejoice over the good ones.' "

Soon it's time for Herrigel to move back to Europe, bringing home with him what he has learned and also his bow. In a section that fascinates me, his master takes some shots with Herrigel's bow, but urges him not to let others use it. The bow remembers.

When it's time to leave for good, Herrigel is anxious that he will forget all he has learned.

"When I asked the Master how we could get on without him on our return to Europe, he said: 'Your question is already answered by the fact that I made you take a test. You have now reached a stage where teacher and pupil are no longer two persons, but one. You can separate from me any time you wish. Even if broad seas lie between us, I shall always be with you when you practice what you have learned.' "

Herrigel realizes that the lessons apply to other areas of life.

"What is true of archery and swordsmanship also applies to all the other arts. Thus, mastery in ink-painting is only attained when the hand, exercising perfect control over technique, executes what hovers before the mind's eye at the same moment when the mind begins to form it, without there being a hair's breadth between. Painting then becomes spontaneous calligraphy. Here again the painter's instructions might be: spend ten years observing bamboos, become a bamboo yourself, then forget everything and—paint."

I've tried archery. I am dismal at it. The only time I ever hit a bull's-eye, it was the wrong one; I actually missed my target by such a wide margin that I hit a fellow archer's target with a perfect bull's-eye. It's a wonder I didn't kill anyone. I put down my bow before I did and have never taken it up again.

So I decided to take the author at his word and attempt to apply what I learned in this book to my favorite endeavor: reading. And in doing so, I've come to believe that reading most certainly is an art. Schools often tend, however, to teach it as a skill, drumming into little heads the alphabet and getting kids addicted to phonics. We acknowledge different speeds and different levels of comprehension and different types of reading—shallow versus deep. But essentially, reading is regarded as something dichotomous. If people ask you if you can read, they are expecting a yes or no answer.

But I believe it's far more complicated and simple than that: every time you read, you are learning how to read. Reading is an art we practice our whole lives. It's not like tying a shoe—it's like ink painting or flower arranging or, yes, archery. Some writers make it easier for us to practice this art, and some more difficult. Every writer teaches us how to read; every book teaches us how to read; we teach ourselves how to read. The more we read, the better at reading we become. At the end of each page I'm a better reader than I was at the start.

All of which is to say, there is only one way to practice the art of reading—and that's to read.

Lin Yutang also believed that reading is an art. One chapter of *The Importance of Living* is devoted to "The Art of Reading." Lin writes that "The man who has not the habit of reading is imprisoned in his immediate world, in respect to time and space. His life falls into a set routine; he is limited to contact and conversation with a few friends and acquaintances, and he sees only what happens in his immediate neighborhood."

On the practical side, Lin believed that reading gives us "charm and flavor," but he was careful to caution against reading for our own good. "Anyone who reads a book with a sense of obligation does not understand the art of reading."

He quotes the ancient scholar Yüan Chunglang, "You can leave the books that you don't like alone, *and let other people read them.*"

And he follows with this admonition: "There can be, therefore, no books that one absolutely must read. For our intellectual interests grow like a tree or flow like a river. So long as there is proper sap, the tree will grow anyhow, and so long as there is fresh current from the spring, the water will flow."

Near the end of *The Importance of Living* comes a section where Lin presents the wisdom of Chang Ch'ao, a mid-seventeenth-century writer, beloved for his literary maxims. Here is Chang Ch'ao on reading at different times in your life: "Reading books in one's youth is like looking at the moon through a crevice; reading books in middle age is like looking at the moon in one's courtyard; and reading books in old age is like looking at the moon on an open terrace. This is because the depth of benefits of reading varies in proportion to the depth of one's own experience."

For Lin, reading is an act "consisting of two sides, the author and the reader." And Lin believed that choosing a favorite author is no small thing—it's epic, as epic as finding the right master to teach you the art of archery.

"I regard the discovery of one's favorite author," Lin writes, "as the most critical event in one's intellectual development. . . . One has to be independent and search out his masters. Who is one's favorite author, no one can tell, probably not even the man himself. It is like love at first sight. The reader cannot be told to love this one or that one, but when he has found the author he loves, he knows it himself by a kind of instinct."

Finally, Lin turns to the appropriate time and place for

reading: "There is no proper place and time for reading. When the mood for reading comes, one can read anywhere. If one knows the enjoyment of reading, he will read in school or out of school, and in spite of all schools . . .

"What, then, is the true art of reading? The simple answer is to just take up a book and read when the mood comes. To be thoroughly enjoyed, reading must be entirely spontaneous."

And that's how you master archery.

Song of Solomon
Admiring Greatness

I HAD A FRIEND who read more voraciously than anyone I've ever met, not just after he retired but throughout his entire life. He had been a playwright and a college professor, and he loved books passionately. But he was also one of the most vigorous and adventuresome people I've ever known, with a life that took him from service in naval intelligence in Morocco and Europe during World War II to travels all over the world. He was a strong swimmer, who loved the water. He was classically handsome, wickedly funny, charmingly contrarian, and profoundly smart, though he wore that quality so lightly he made everyone around him feel smart as well. He was my whole family's best friend and had friends of all ages and backgrounds. Right up to his very last days, he maintained a voluminous correspondence with dozens of people around the world, a never-ending stream of postcards and letters. He also kept a typed diary, from his teens until he died. And he took and saved thousands of photographs.

Throughout the first half century or so of his life, my friend amassed a great collection of books, many thousands of volumes. But when he reached the age of about seventy, he began to sell or give away almost all his books. And as he began to approach eighty, he decided that he would henceforth keep exactly one hundred books. For many people, that's still a lot of books. But to a lifelong book lover and retired professor, that's hardly any at all. To keep his collection this small, he devised a rule for himself: he could keep a book he had recently read only if he gave one of his hundred away.

This friend died in his early eighties, shortly after suffering a stroke. The one hundred volumes he left behind gave those of us who loved him a remarkable portrait of his life: an autobiography composed not of sentences but of books. Because he loved to travel, works by Isabella Bird, Sir Wilfred Thesiger, and Jan Morris were on his shelf. Because he loved Morocco, books by Jane Bowles, Paul Bowles, and Mohamed Mrabet were there, too. He was a scholar of George Bernard Shaw. So he had cheated a bit: the six-volume *Bernard Shaw: Complete Plays with Prefaces* was allowed to count as one book among the hundred. And there were also books of photography, including *Diane Arbus: Revelations*.

Many of the books were fairly eccentric—not what the world generally regards as great works, but ones that held meaning for my friend. A love for martinis required that he keep several books on the history of that classic cocktail. A lifelong obsession with the French Foreign Legion meant that a first edition of the 1924 novel *Beau Geste* by P. C. Wren remained one of his treasured volumes. Not many other novels survived on the shelves, but among the few that did was *Song of Solomon* by Toni Morrison.

I remember talking with him over the years about *Song of Solomon*, at first when I was studying it in college. He had read it a few years before that, soon after it was published in 1977.

Song of Solomon was Morrison's third novel. In 1993, after her sixth, she was awarded the Nobel Prize in Literature. The citation from the Swedish Academy read: Awarded to Toni Morrison, "who, in novels characterized by visionary force and poetic import, gives life to an essential aspect of American reality." Rita Dove, former Poet Laureate of the United States, described Morrison in a 2015 speech before the National Book Critics Circle as "not only a prose virtuoso but also a master of poetic sensibilities and lyrical language: Her influence on discourse, idiom and the vernacular has transformed our perception of the intricate paths to the interior consciousness."

I envy anyone who has yet to read *Song of Solomon*. I will never forget my first reading of it, the growing tightness in my chest and throat, page after page.

At the heart of this novel is the migration of a character named Milkman Dead from north to south, the opposite of the twentieth century's "Great Migration" of African Americans from the rural south to the cities of the north. And images of flight are present throughout—flight as escape from peril, and as a symbol of freedom; flight by foot and through the air. *Song of Solomon* is a novel of characters in motion.

Rereading the novel, I noticed something that had barely registered in my prior readings, and that is the role that a particular book plays in the life of Pilate, Milkman's aunt. One of the unusual things about Pilate is that she has no navel, for which she is often shunned, forcing her to leave one place after another. She travels with almost nothing: just some rocks, a spool of thread, and one book—a geography book—that not only accompanies her but guides her.

But even when not forced to leave, she grows restless and feels compelled to move along, from one place to another: "It was as if her geography book had marked her to roam the country, planting her feet in each pink, yellow, blue or green state."

Just one book, opening up the world.

Remembering my friend and his one hundred books got me thinking about what books would make the cut should I ever decide to limit my own library in the same way. Even if I could have only ten books, *Song of Solomon* would be among them. It was at the top of the list I recommended to that West Point cadet on our turbulent flight to Las Vegas.

The apartment my husband and I share is stuffed with books. We both collect books. Everywhere. Every table is a bookshelf. The floor is also a bookshelf. To walk from one place to another requires navigating between piles of books stacked precariously, one on top of another, without regard to shape or size.

Whenever I knock over a stack, the thought of the zero-sum bookshelf becomes especially appealing.

But it's not just for reasons of space. (I also sometimes read books on an e-reader, and there is certainly no reason to delete any book from my library there.) There's something challenging—in a good way—about trying to compose your own one-hundred-book library. It forces you to figure what matters to you most. I love the British radio program *Desert Island Discs*, where the guest has to explain what eight records she or he would take to a desert island. Choosing your one-hundred-book library is like *Desert Island Discs* on steroids, with books in place of albums.

I love my odd, eccentric books, just as my friend loved his. They are part of who I am, and many of them have earned a permanent place on my shelf—even if I later decide that shelf can contain only one hundred volumes. And I like my mediocre pleasures, too—modest books that I will pass along once I'm done so someone else can enjoy them, too.

But when I look over at my copy of *Song of Solomon* (which sits on a proper shelf, not on the floor), I remember what it feels like to read something truly great, which often inspires me to search for books that can hold a place beside it.

A Little Life
Hugging

I READ Hanya Yanagihara's novel *A Little Life* in three days. It's a long novel, but I was so involved in the lives of the characters, I felt for them so keenly, that I didn't want to stop reading. I barely ate; I didn't answer the phone; I didn't check my emails. People often talk about reading a book feverishly. This was that—I was not quite myself when reading it, a little delirious. When I got close to the end, I called in sick to work so I could finish. When I was finally done, I wanted—I needed—to talk to others who had read it. One friend told me that all she wanted after finishing was a hug. I didn't want a hug; I wanted to talk. But that's because I'm not a hugger.

The world is filled now with huggers. Maybe that's because we live in such a technological age that people crave human touch. Men and women whom you barely know hug you hello and goodbye. Kids in school hug each other. Even in business meetings, people will give you a hug if they've sat with you in meetings a few times before (though not if they work at the same company). I really don't like being hugged by anyone other than my husband. People regard this as a character flaw. One friend even devoted an hour of time with his analyst to discussing why I didn't like to hug. I gather he takes it personally.

Whenever I see reports about the autism spectrum, one of the symptoms frequently mentioned is aversion to touch. And I can see how, if taken to an extreme, this aversion could be hugely problematic. But it's also natural that some people like less contact than others. And we shouldn't be forced to embrace when we don't want to. Or be judged hostile or cold. You can be a warm abstainer from hugging just as you can be a chilly hugger.

Lin Yutang wasn't a hugger, either. He wasn't even a handshaker. In a chapter called "Some Curious Western Customs," he rails against shaking hands. "Of all the ridiculous Western customs, I think that of shaking hands is one of the worst . . . I object to this custom for hygienic and many other reasons." He starts with the hygiene—the consumptive coughing of a stranger into his own hand and then that person stretching it out to grasp yours—and continues on to the whole question of how you are supposed to divine the character of your new acquaintance by the way she or he shakes your hand. "Some novelists profess that you can tell a man's character from his type of handshake, distinguishing between the assertive, the retiring, the dishonest and the weak and clammy hands which instinctively repel one.

I wish to be spared the trouble of analyzing a person's moral character every time I have to meet him, or reading from the degree of his pressure the increase or decrease of his affection towards me."

I never thought about hugging much until I read Edward T. Hall's *The Hidden Dimension*. Hall was a cultural anthropologist who worked both in universities and for the state department, advising diplomats who were about to be posted abroad. One of Hall's great insights was that attitudes toward personal space are both personal and cultural. In Italy, for example, he observed that people stand very close to one another when they talk. In America, or in pre-hugging America, they tend to keep more distance in similar situations. He describes an Italian and an American at a cocktail party with the Italian essentially chasing the American around the room as the American tries to keep a certain distance between them and the Italian seeks to close the gap.

Hall also points out other areas where cultures differ when it comes to how we feel about the space we inhabit. For example, he notes that Germans tend to work with their office doors closed. An open office door in Germany means you aren't working. Americans, on the other hand, work with them open. A closed door means something sensitive or secret is being discussed—or that people are conspiring. So when Germans and Americans work together—in a traditional workplace with separate offices—the Americans think the Germans are conspiring against them, and the Germans think the Americans are goofing off.

Hall had earlier described how animals naturally space themselves with precision—for example, birds in flight. He described how if you crowd animals even slightly it causes them to become vicious and to turn on one another. And how something as simple as the placement of furniture in a room or public space changes what happens in it. Hall contrasts the lack of conversation in "spaces such as railway waiting rooms in which the seating provisions are formally arranged in fixed rows" with the way that the "tables in a European sidewalk cafe tend to bring people together."

In a chapter near the middle of this book, Hall turns toward the language of space—and then the literature of space. He writes, "Writers, like painters, are often concerned with space. Their success in communicating perception depends upon the use of visual and other clues to convey *different* degrees of closeness. In light of all that had been done with language, it seemed possible, therefore, that a study of literature might produce data on space perception against which I could check information obtained from other sources." He goes on to present passages from *King Lear*, Henry David Thoreau's *Walden*, Samuel Butler's *The Way of All Flesh*, from Mark Twain, Saint-Exupéry, Nobel Prize winner Yasunari Kawabata, and Franz Kafka.

Here is the passage he quotes from *Walden:*

One inconvenience I sometimes experienced in so small a house, was the difficulty of getting to a sufficient distance from my guest when we began to utter the big thoughts in big words. You want room for your thoughts to get into sailing trim and run a course or two before they make their port. The bullet of your thought must have overcome its lateral and ricochet motion and fallen into its last and steady course before it reaches the ear of the hearer, else it may plough out again through the side of his head. Also our sentences wanted room to unfold and form their columns in the interval. Individuals, like nations, must have suitable broad and natural boundaries, even a considerable neutral ground, between them . . . In my house we were so near that we could not begin to hear. . . . If we are merely loquacious and loud talkers, then we can afford to stand very near together, cheek by jowl, and feel each other's breath; but if we speak reservedly and thoughtfully we want to be farther apart, that all animal heat and moisture may have a chance to evaporate.

Hall cites this as confirmation of points he's made earlier, writing of Thoreau, "His sensitivity to the need to stay outside the olfactory and thermal zones (the zones within which one can smell breath and feel the heat from another's body), and his pushing against the wall to get more space in which to voice the big thought, point up some of the unconscious distance-sensing and distance-setting mechanisms."

We all have these mechanisms—and they are deeply programmed by culture and nature and nurture. We move differently through space. Some of us swagger—like frat-boy athletes leaping up against each other to bump chests—and carry on through the day with the same bold conviction that we have the right to take up not just the area we occupy but the air all around us. On the subway, in airplanes, in parks, I'm always amazed at the way that some people, usually but not always men, command the area around them: with spread legs or splayed elbows or outstretched feet. Others shrink back into themselves, always finding their way to the edge of the room, the last row, avoiding concerts and ball games and places where they are certain to bump up against others.

Hall also includes an extraordinary passage from Samuel Butler's novel *The Way of All Flesh*, in which a mother uses proximity to extract a confession from her son. By sitting close to him, "*taking hold of his hand* and placing it within her own," she has him just where she wants him and needs him to be. As she strokes his hair, he becomes guilt-ridden and anxious—and he winces, something his mother sees right away. Proximity is love and danger. As Hall has earlier pointed out, the lion mounts a stool simply because it is in his path as he is stalking a trainer who has invaded the lion's personal space. This personal space can be measured in centimeters—Hall calls it "critical distance." One step closer and the lion would leap for the trainer's throat. One step back, and the lion stays on the stool.

In *A Little Life*, Hanya Yanagihara writes about four friends, following them from right after college until well into middle age. The two most extreme characters are at the opposite ends of the spectrum when it comes to touch and space. One, JB, an artist, is an ebullient space-taker; the other, Jude, a lawyer, is a man who can't bear to be touched. Over the course of the novel, Jude at times allows people close and at other times withdraws. Jude's dearest friend is Willem, an actor. The author writes of one time when Willem saw Jude and "reached over and hugged him very close, which he knew Jude didn't like but which he had already decided he would start doing anyway." And later, again about Jude, that "he was more skittish than ever about being touched, especially . . . by [his mentor] Harold; a month ago, when Harold had visited, Jude had practically danced out of the way to keep Harold from hugging him." Harold and Willem recognize that Jude can't help this. In the latter scene, Willem feels so bad for Harold when Harold's hug is rejected by Jude that Willem walks over and gives Harold a hug.

A Little Life is one of the most engrossing books I've ever read, and also one of the most upsetting. Over the course of the novel you learn about the horrific physical and sexual abuse Jude endured as a child, abuse that has so scarred him that he feels compelled to continue to scar himself. In fact, Jude is covered with scars—from his childhood and from his own mutilations. He's also broken inside—convinced that he's repulsive in every way. The reader, however, knows that he's beautiful. And that he's strong. The reader learns his story long before any of his three best friends do. Much of the suspense comes from waiting to see if he can ever open up and share with them something of his life. There's also a defining incident from his childhood that is shared with the reader only at the very end.

It's a novel that asks very big questions about our ability to escape our pasts. But as much as it tells a tale of incredible pain and suffering, it's also a story of the transformative and sustaining power of friendship. There is an adoption that had me sobbing—happily. And then there's an accident that wrecked me completely.

When we say a work of art has an emotional effect on us, we frequently say it *touched* us. Or it *moved* us. That is, it invaded our space or caused us to change our space.

Ultimately, one of the things that I found most moving in *A Little Life* was the way Jude's friends wrestled with his desire *not* to be touched and tolerated for decades his determination, healthy or not, to keep his story to himself. When should we interfere in the lives of our friends? What are the privileges of pain? When is withdrawal self-preservation and when is it emotional blackmail? These are just some of the questions the novel raises.

We all need space. Some of us need it more than others. For some, like Jude, there's a powerful reason. For others, like me, it's simply the way we're wired, part of who we are.

Edward T. Hall doesn't make value judgments. He just observes. In the animal kingdom, he writes, "Some species huddle together and require physical contact with each other. Others completely avoid touching. No apparent logic governs the category into which a species falls. Contact creatures include the walrus, the hippopotamus, the pig, the brown bat, the parakeet, and the hedgehog among many other species. The horse, the dog, the cat, the rat, the muskrat, the hawk, and the blackheaded gull are non-contact species. Curiously enough, closely related animals may belong to different categories. The great Emperor penguin is a contact species . . . The smaller Adelie penguin is a non-contact species."

Admittedly, I am a non-contact creature, and yet books have shown me time and again that you don't need corporality to touch someone. If you go to give me a hug, I might react somewhat like Jude—for no better reason than Lin Yutang cited when explaining his aversion to handshaking. But if you tell me a heartfelt story, in person or in print, you can touch me.

Bird by Bird
Feeling Sensitive

I WAS ONCE spending time with a friend who suddenly announced, "I'm bored and I'm angry." I asked her why she'd blurted that out. She told me that she was bored sitting around with me and angry because she'd wanted to go for a walk and no one had wanted to go with her. I thought her honesty was terrific. At that moment, I was reminded of a college friend who had taken a life course called Direct Centering, which soon proved to be a scary cult. She proudly announced that, thanks to this program, she could now tell people exactly how she felt about them. If she was angry, she could tell them so; if she felt a sexual attraction, she could also say that. Luckily, I was off the hook on both counts: she was neither attracted to me nor angry with me.

I wanted to ask her what she would do if she was both angry with and sexually attracted to the same person at the same time. What would she say? I also was curious as to whether there were any emotions other than rage and lust that were permissible; there didn't seem to be.

When I compared my two friends I had a realization: It's always useful to know what others are feeling, but sometimes it's not a bad idea to keep your feelings to yourself.

Much of life is spent trying to divine the emotions of those around us. I texted someone an hour ago and I haven't heard back. Does that mean she's mad at me? I thought her phone message was a bit abrupt, and I always "like" her posts on Facebook and she never "likes" mine back. Did I do something wrong? They didn't invite me over and they invited everyone else. Do we have a problem? Was she giving me the stink-eye? Why does he now sign his emails "Best" when it used to be "Warmest"?

And we spend much of life quietly simmering; we want to share but we don't, for fear of sounding peevish or petty or just because we prefer to sulk in silence. We've also all probably been burned at one time or another when we *have* expressed our feelings. (Hollywood loves to make a certain kind of movie where a character suddenly can only tell the truth. Chaos ensues. Just watch *Liar Liar*, a 1997 Jim Carrey movie about a lawyer who suddenly finds himself unable to lie, for one example of this genre.)

We communicate with one another far more frequently than we ever have before, giving occasion for hundreds more daily interactions, each ripe for misinterpretation.

So what to do? How to walk the line between boorish indifference to others and living in a state of constant anxiety about whether we have or haven't offended, between letting others know how we are feeling and burdening them with information they don't need or want?

When it comes to these kinds of questions, I often turn to Anne Lamott for guidance. I've gained more practical wisdom from her nine nonfiction books than I have from any other living writer. In her nonfiction she blends memoir and advice, chronicling the evolution of her own Christian faith, her journey through addiction and sobriety, and how she came to create community and family along the way—and she tells readers frankly what she's been taught and what she had to learn. She's written books about the death of her father from cancer, her son's first year, and being a grandmother to her son's son. She's told stories about her friends' lives with cancer and ALS. And she tells you exactly how she feels.

Lamott's book *Bird by Bird: Some Instructions on Writing and Life* is one of the few books I read once every few years. It has lots of advice that's seemingly aimed at writers: about writing shitty (pardon the French, as my grandmother used to say) first drafts (just to get something down on paper); about the danger of perfectionism; about how you are going to be jealous of more successful authors, and you just have to deal with that. But, as promised in the subtitle, just about all of the advice applies not only to writing but also to life.

One of the most useful bits of wisdom comes in the story Lamott tells to explain why she gave this book its odd title:

> Thirty years ago my older brother, who was ten years old at the time, was trying to get a report on birds written that he'd had three months to write, which was due the next day. We were out at our family cabin in Bolinas, and he was

at the kitchen table close to tears, surrounded by binder paper and pencils and unopened books on birds, immobilized by the hugeness of the task ahead. Then my father sat down beside him, put his arm around my brother's shoulder, and said, "Bird by bird, buddy. Just take it bird by bird."

So whenever I'm thinking that a task is too big to tackle, or that I've procrastinated so much that it's no longer possible, I think of Anne and her older brother and their father—and then I start to work on it bird by bird. Clean our apartment (which often resembles a frat house, boxer shorts and dirty mugs strewn everywhere) because there are guests coming in an hour? How to get that done? Bird by bird. Or, rather: boxer by boxer.

Anne Lamott walks readers through moral and spiritual and practical dilemmas in her life and the lives of others, mostly people she knows but also people she's read about in books and seen on the news. As she explores her life and theirs, she gives me a map for walking through my own. When my mother was dying of cancer, we both found ourselves turning to *Traveling Mercies: Some Thoughts on Faith*, which we'd first read when it came out in 1999. Lamott writes that the two best prayers are quite simple: "Help me, help me, help me," and "Thank you, thank you, thank you." I used both again and again during my mother's last months, though I also wasn't above asking for more specific blessings, like a few more months with my mother.

In a more recent book, *Help, Thanks, Wow: The Three Essential Prayers*, she added a third prayer: the "Wow" that is the last word of the title. This is the prayer that helps you acknowledge all the wonder and blessings around: petals in spring; a Georgia O'Keeffe painting in a museum; a dance by Fred Astaire or Pina Bausch. There are "lowercase wows"— like "clean sheets after a hard day." And "uppercase Wows. Yosemite. Fireworks." Whether something is upper- or lowercase or a wow at all depends on us. I try to be aware of the "Wow" prayer at least once a day but usually forget. It's much easier to remember to pray when life is going badly, or we've just been given a gift, than simply to stop from time to time to acknowledge how much awesomeness is often around us.

It's not just what Anne Lamott says but how she says it. I love her voice on the page, her honesty: she's brisk but warm, wry but tender. She's my senior by only eight years, but she has a kind of hard-won wisdom that I associate with certain much-older elders I've encountered at key moments in my life. More than anything, she reminds me of my grandmother's friend Alice who used four-letter words (out of my grandmother's earshot) and could swallow a wooden matchstick and bring it back up again. I could always count on Alice to tell me the truth, tell it to me straight, listen to whatever I had to say, and never blow my cover on anything. That's Anne Lamott.

Actually, Alice was probably the same age then as Anne Lamott is now. Funny, that. To my ten-year-old self, Alice seemed ancient, as I must now to the youngest people in my life.

Anne Lamott can write like nobody's business or, rather, everybody's. One minute you are smiling at a vivid image—her description of herself at the start of *Bird by Bird* as a little girl walking around with "my shoulders up to my ears, like Richard Nixon." Then she throws in a joke or two—about how she was clearly the child most likely to become a serial killer or have "dozens and dozens of cats." But right after she moves in for the kill: "Instead I got funny. I got funny because boys, older boys I didn't even know, would ride by on their bicycles and taunt me about my weird looks. Each time felt like a drive-by shooting. I think this is why I walked like Nixon: I think I was trying to plug my ears with my shoulders, but they wouldn't quite reach."

Lamott's father was a writer, and she wanted to be one, too. She realized that "one of the gifts of being a writer is that it gives you an excuse to do things, to go places and explore. Another is that writing motivates you to look closely at life, at life as it lurches by and tramps around." Lamott's father believed that writing—like reading—teaches you how to pay attention. You would need to be sensitive in order to become the kind of writer that Anne Lamott is; but you could also say that the kind of writing that she does will make you more sensitive.

Sadly, sensitivity isn't universally regarded as a good quality. For children, it's okay—just as long as you aren't labeled "oversensitive," as Lamott was. In one of her recent books, *Stitches: A Handbook on Meaning, Hope and Repair*, published in 2013, Lamott writes about this:

If you were raised in the 1950s or 1960s, and grasped how scary the world could be, in Birmingham, Vietnam and the house on the corner where the daddy drank, you were diagnosed as being the overly sensitive child. There were entire books written on the subject of the overly sensitive child. What the term meant was that you noticed how unhappy or crazy your parents were. Also, you worried about global starvation, animals at the pound who didn't get adopted, and smog. What a nut. You looked into things too deeply, and you noticed things that not many others could see, and this exasperated your parents and teachers. They said, "You need to have thicker skin!" That would have been excellent, but you couldn't go buy thicker skin at the five-and-dime.

Any healthy half-awake person is occasionally going to be pierced with a sense of the unfairness and the catastrophe of life for ninety-five percent of the people on this earth. However, if you reacted, or cried, or raised the subject at all, you were being a worrywart.

For adults, the label "oversensitive" is rarely used, because, in most quarters, when people speak of an adult as being "sensitive" they almost always mean it pejoratively; the prefix "over" is redundant. "Sensitive" is bad all by itself; "sensitive" is code for *over*sensitive. Any kind of concern someone might raise in, say, an office setting can be dismissed with the accusation that the "complainer" is just being "sensitive" for raising it. This is especially true if the person who is raising the concern is not in the majority. Problems not experienced by the majority are often not seen as problems at all, and if they are, they are certainly no one's fault; the fault is in the receiver's too-sensitive antennae. "You're just being sensitive" means "You are complaining about something everyone else thinks is trivial." And that simply means "You are complaining about something that concerns you and not us, because we really don't care about you."

Sometimes when I've been accused of being sensitive, I've crumbled. Sometimes, I've doubled down, arguing my point. You can try to explain why something so small to others is so big to you, and you may succeed, or not.

But often encounters aren't even that clear-cut. Someone will voice a concern, and others may acknowledge it, but has anyone really heard? Has anything changed?

So the questions remain—when to say how we feel and when to keep it to ourselves; when are we being sensitive and when too sensitive?

In *Stitches*, Lamott writes, "I wish there were shortcuts to wisdom and self-knowledge: cuter abysses or three-day spa wilderness experiences. Sadly, it doesn't work that way. I so resent this."

I'm glad Anne Lamott told me she resents this. I resent it, too.

Rebecca
Betraying

TELEPHONE. Telegraph. Or Tell Terry.

I have never known anyone who gossiped as much as my friend Terry. I met him in the mid-1980s and learned within hours that any comment I made to Terry would be broadcast to a wide audience of friends and acquaintances and strangers. I can't quite remember how Terry came into my life: he was the ex-boyfriend of a friend's ex-boyfriend, I think. What makes it hard to remember is all the gossip: Terry was constantly at war with one person or another in our circle for repeating something he shouldn't have to someone he shouldn't have.

I would love to write that there was nothing malicious about Terry's gossiping, but that wouldn't be true. There was often something malicious about it; he was the little boy at the party who switches the sugar and salt just to see the expression on people's faces as they sip their salted tea. But there was also something infectious about it; it allowed us all to partake but not indulge—we could pass on what Terry told us in the guise of another Terry story: Can you believe what Terry did this time around?

Terry's parties were almost always gossip-worthy. He lived in a 1960s high-rise in the unfashionable far-east Upper East Side of Manhattan and would cram up to a hundred people into an apartment that could comfortably fit thirty or forty. Terry had immigrated to New York from Singapore by way of boarding school in Australia, and he worked in fashion. His friends included Singapore expats, East Village gallerists, Australian rugby players, assistants from fashion magazines, and an assortment of other characters. Terry stood barely five foot five and had a round face, so that even when very thin he looked pudgy. The other feature everyone noticed when meeting Terry was his fangs; he had canine teeth so sharp and prominent that they always seemed in danger of piercing his lower lip.

When I first met Terry, he was sometimes drunk. In later years, he was often drunk. And then he was always drunk. He carried everywhere an enormous satchel, filled with books and scarves and who knows what else. I always suspected that there was at least a fifth of vodka buried within, if not a liter bottle. When I first met Terry, he worked for a fashion house. In later years, he started his own company making the most beautiful vests I've ever seen and will ever see, fantastic handmade vests of peacock feathers and colorful woven ribbon, vests that became for a while in the mid-nineties the hot item for grooms to wear at weddings around the world.

Then he made dresses for private clients. But the financial crisis made customers scarce. And then I can't remember him working at all, except to make garments for friends.

Terry loved to talk on the phone. And he called at the worst possible moments: just as a friend was arriving; just as you were sitting down to dinner; just as you were leaving late on your way to a movie. My friendship with Terry predated caller ID, and I signed up for the service partly because of Terry. It allowed me to screen his calls. He would rarely leave a message; I would see on my caller ID that he was calling and would only sometimes pick up. I usually told myself I would call right back. And I often did. But I often didn't.

Terry's fabulous life became particularly evident on his Facebook posts. He was an early adopter and took to it enthusiastically. He chronicled foods he was cooking and the ingredients he was using (oysters and *uni* and monkfish livers and fresh baby-goat ribs); a high-school reunion; his wanderings around his neighborhood; friends asking for too many favors (free alterations being extremely irritating to him); a case of champagne showing up unlabeled and his having no idea who had sent it. He also put up posts about migraines, weight loss, and visitors acting like vultures, all relayed in a funny-bitchy-exaggerated tone. We went from seeing each other every month or so, to every few months, and then to two or three times a year.

The last time I saw Terry it was for dim sum; he showed up early. Terry was always early, especially to a party, and always the last to leave, to the point where you finally had to escort him out, having washed the dishes, cleaned up the room, returned the furniture to its preparty position, and even having brushed your teeth—Terry would not leave a party until you left him no alternative.

I wish I had better memories of that dim sum lunch, but all I remember is that Terry was drunk. It was 10:00 a.m., and Terry was clearly smashed, slurring his words. He proudly announced that he'd had a big night last night and had started the day with vodka, to take the edge off.

After that, we communicated on Facebook for a few months—he liked some things I posted and I liked some he posted, and we messaged each other that we had to get together. And then a few months went by, and I didn't notice we hadn't been in touch. And then a friend called and told me that Terry was dead—that, essentially, he drank himself to death. Terry had stopped eating and just drank; by the time he checked into a hospital for an infection, he was too far gone to save and didn't seem to want to be saved anyway.

The same friend called later to tell me about the memorial service she was helping to organize. It would be in the staid Frank E. Campbell funeral parlor on upper Madison Avenue, on a Saturday—and my husband, David, and I already had plans to be out of town. It was obviously going to be thronged; no one would notice whether we were there or not, so we decided to go away for the weekend, as planned. As we were heading out Friday evening to catch a train, though, we changed our minds. After all, Terry had been a very good friend. So we called our hosts and made our apologies.

The next day found us arriving early at Frank E. Campbell—as long as we were going, we wanted to be sure to get a seat. The chapels aren't huge there, and we didn't want to have to stand in the back. David wore a vest Terry had designed for him—black and white satin woven into a broad checkerboard.

The first thing that greeted us was a picture of Terry, wearing the very same vest, looking plump and happy and devilish, as always. And then we walked into the chapel to find twenty or so people sitting in pews that could fit more than one hundred. And we twenty or so were the only people who showed up. A dozen of the twenty were Terry's family, from Singapore and Washington, D.C. Then there were fewer than a dozen friends, including the two of us. And there was Terry, in an open casket at the front, looking nothing like the Terry I knew and remembered.

In *Epitaph of a Small Winner*, the narrator (who, as you will recall, is telling the story of his life from beyond the grave) relates the story of the funeral of a young girl, who died at age nineteen. The girl's father is named Damasceno, and the narrator tells us of a conversation he had with him. Cotrim was the girl's uncle.

> As I have not related the death, I shall also omit the seventh-day Mass. A fortnight later I was talking with Damasceno, who was still deeply sad and inconsolable.

He said that the great sorrow with which God had pun-
ished him was increased by the sorrow that man had
inflicted upon him. He did not explain. Three weeks later
he returned to the subject and confided in me that, in the
throes of the irreparable tragedy, he had hoped for the
consolation that the presence of friends can give. Only
twelve people, and three-fourths of them friends of Cotrim,
accompanied his daughter's coffin to the cemetery. And he
had sent out eighty invitations. I expressed the opinion
that there were so many deaths during the epidemic that
one might well excuse the apparent neglect. Damasceno
shook his head sadly and incredulously.

"No," he groaned. "They let me down."

Cotrim, who was present, said:

"Those came who had a genuine interest in you and in
us. The eighty would have come only as a formality, would
have talked about the inertia of the government, about
patent medicines, about the price of real estate, or about
each other . . ."

Damasceno listened in silence, shook his head again,
and sighed:

"But they should at least have come."

That passage would find me later. But on this day, another
graveside speech echoed in my head: Linda Loman's, from
Arthur Miller's *Death of a Salesman*, with her famous phrase,
"Attention must be paid," which she repeats as she mourns
the death of her husband and the world that moved past him.

There were only a few eulogies, but they captured Terry. One of the friends, who had stuck with him through everything, as we later learned, talked of meeting him at Evelyne's, a very hip place in the eighties that was a watering spot for downtown celebrities: the Warhol set, actors, and newly famous East Village artists. Terry had been a waiter there in his early New York years and was legendarily rude. Thus, he became something of a cult figure, with people vying to be served by him and trading stories of what he had said to them. He even barked at Lauren Bacall for keeping her sunglasses on inside.

I think Terry would have loved that this story was told at his service. Or the Terry I first met would have loved it. I realize now that the Terry of later years was too unhappy to get much pleasure out of anything. In fact, the Terry of later years might have been the loneliest person I've ever known.

On his Facebook page, Terry listed his favorite films—in the number one spot was *All About Eve*, a movie beloved for its acid-tipped quips. Also *Midnight Cowboy*, an ode to urban alienation, and *Goodbye, Mr. Chips*, made from James Hilton's moving novel about a beloved boarding-school teacher. For Terry, boarding school was a golden time: he was comrades with everyone, even the most rugged of the jocks. They were a family of friends, and he was the beloved impish young brother.

Terry and I would talk about books from time to time, when we weren't talking about food. We both agreed that

A Fine Balance by Rohinton Mistry is one of the greatest books of all time. He loved the very eerie novel *Picnic at Hanging Rock* by Joan Lindsay, as do I. *Valley of the Dolls* by Jacqueline Susann was among his favorites; he quoted from it frequently. That was exactly the book one would have expected him to like: campy, wicked, packed with pill-popping models. On his Facebook page, Terry listed Susann's classic alongside books by great gay authors: E. M. Forster and Gore Vidal and Truman Capote and Patrick Dennis, famous for *Auntie Mame*. I wasn't surprised that he loved Robert Hughes's *The Fatal Shore*, a masterful history of Australia. That was in keeping with his nostalgia for his school years. Evelyn Waugh's achingly nostalgic *Brideshead Revisited* was another book he adored; he reread it almost every year.

Nor was I surprised when Terry told me that he loved *Rebecca* by Daphne du Maurier, that sinister romance of resentment and deception. Terry was gothic at heart.

This book was first published in 1938, one year after Lin Yutang's *The Importance of Living*. But it is a very different response to the uncertainties and anxieties of the time. It's a book about scheming, duplicity, insecurity, and murder—and it ends in conflagration.

With its famous first line ("Last night I dreamt I went to Manderley again"), its unnamed narrator (we know her only as the second Mrs. de Winter and never learn her name), and with its whopper of a twist at the end, du Maurier's novel became one of the bestselling books of all time. Alfred Hitchcock directed a film adaptation, but with a very different ending. It starred Sir Laurence Olivier, Joan Fontaine, and Judith Anderson and won the Academy Award for Best Picture in 1940.

Rebecca is a novel powered by jealousy. The most memorable character is Mrs. Danvers, the housekeeper, one of the great underminers in literature. Devoted to the memory of the first Mrs. de Winter, the Rebecca of the title, she is hell-bent on destroying the second. Mrs. Danvers is a baleful presence, and she preys upon the insecurities of our narrator. One of the pivotal scenes involves a dress—Mrs. Danvers suggests to the naïve and trusting second Mrs. de Winter that she attend a costume ball in a gown that the housekeeper knows will enrage Maxim de Winter by reminding him of his first wife, who has been dead for only a year. No surprise that Terry loved a book where a gown is at once a garment and a weapon.

But *Rebecca* is also a book about loneliness. Loneliness reaches into every corner of Manderley, the de Winter seaside estate. Its endless driveway leads through dark woods to a shocking wall of bloodred rhododendrons, and the stone house behind the wall is described as "secretive and silent."

Our narrator is soon desperately lonely, lonely enough to try to kill herself. Maxim is lonely, too, though not for the reasons we at first think. And as cruel as Mrs. Danvers is, she is also terribly alone. (Although she is called "Mrs." and not "Miss," she has never been married—that was just a convention of the time when it came to housekeepers.) She had looked after Rebecca "for years before she married and practically brought her up." Rebecca was the great and only love of her life.

Halfway through the novel, Maxim says to the second Mrs. de Winter, "We're not meant for happiness, you and I." I suspect this quote would have resonated with Terry, especially in his last months.

Of all the people I've known who have died, Terry is the one whose memory fills me with the deepest regret. Did I need to screen those calls? Would it have killed me to answer and chat, even when I was tired or it was a little late? Couldn't I have seen the desperation behind the blizzard of Facebook posts? I don't kid myself that I could have saved Terry, but I do know I could have seen more of him.

Part of the reason I suspect that Terry's service was so ill attended was that he had genuinely hurt a lot of people; his gossip went from being cute when we were younger to quite vicious later, and he caused a lot of trouble. Terry actively alienated his friends. But my sin? A disappearing act. I was there and then I wasn't, too caught up in my own busy life.

Ultimately, the problem with all our electronic communication is that it is so ill equipped to convey tone. What I read at the time as comic irritation with the world was in retrospect genuine despair. And as for Terry's nostalgia— embodied by the boarding-school fiction and the posts about his Australian boyhood—I fear that was more torture than pleasant ache. I fear that it was the kind of nostalgia that Mr. Tracy had taught us when we read about Odysseus and his desperate need to return to Ithaca: "pain for home."

The friend who told me of Terry's death later described visiting Terry in his last days. He had fallen after checking into the hospital and cracked his head on the floor so loudly that his doctor heard the sound from outside the room. Terry recovered from that, but suffered from nightmares and day terrors, even worse after the fall than before. He continued to refuse to eat and was increasingly jaundiced as his liver failed. The doctor had suggested to this friend that she bring pictures of Terry in happier times when she came to visit. Terry wouldn't look at them; when she tried to pin them on the wall next to his bed, he cried out for her to take them down.

It was particularly painful for her to see Terry refuse food—food had been one of the joys of his life. He was a generous and talented cook; he would show up at Thanksgiving and cook the entire meal for her family, taking great pride each year in turning out a feast more delicious than the last. Terry loved to explain the science—the role of the bay leaf; how to get the turkey to roast just right. His own dinner parties were epic, course after course served from his improbably small galley kitchen: Singapore Chinese food from his youth, the hearty roasts he had grown to love in Australia, delicacies from Europe on which he had spent massive sums, and whatever was most fresh from the New York Greenmarket.

But in the end he only drank: straight vodka. And he was too sick at the very end to watch television or read. Or maybe he didn't want to do either.

Books had nothing to do with Terry's death. But I can't help thinking that they didn't help, either—that the books he loved most helped him romanticize his more cutting characteristics and filled him with longing for a time in his life that he desperately missed.

When I think of Terry, there's nothing I can think of that I would have given him to read. I just wish I had been a better friend.

Reading Lolita in Tehran
Choosing Your Life

I'LL SOMETIMES HEAR someone say of a book, "That book saved my life."

Recently, I came across a story of how a book did literally save a life. Actually, there were several books involved, but one deserves more credit than the others: an Oxford University Press volume on John Wyclif by Stephen Edmund Lahey. The book, published in 2009, explores the cultural and intellectual atmosphere of fourteenth-century Britain in order to give context to the writings of John Wyclif (more often spelled Wycliffe), the philosopher-theologian whose theories were key to Henry VIII's break from Catholicism and whose philosophy helped establish the Anglican church. It's part of a series on great medieval thinkers.

The life this book saved belonged to a twenty-one-year-old Florida State University student named Jason Derfuss, who had the very bad luck to be at the university's library when a mentally ill graduate of the school, with extreme paranoia, started shooting there. Derfuss would later tell an NBC News television network reporter, "There is no way I should be alive." He said that he first heard a loud bang. "I knew it was a gunshot right away and slowly turned around to see the gunman running toward another student and shoot him two times." Before it all was over, the gunman had shot at seven people, including Derfuss, and had injured three of them; one, a twenty-one-year-old student, is now paralyzed from the waist down. Hundreds of students had barricaded themselves in the library or fled in panic; eventually, the gunman was shot dead by police, after he refused to drop his gun. When Derfuss got home, he opened his knapsack. "I pulled out the books and saw that they were all ripped apart. I started examining them and my friend found a bullet in the back page." The bullet had ripped through several books. The one that stopped it cold was the book about Wyclif.

Similarly, a book—or, rather, a book-length manuscript—saved Theodore Roosevelt's life. While Roosevelt was on the campaign trail in October 1912, an assassin shot him twice, but the script for the speech, which was in his overcoat pocket, slowed the bullets. He also had a metal eyeglass case between the shooter and his chest, so that clearly helped, too. Roosevelt was on his way to give the speech when shot, and though he knew he was injured, he realized that the bullet hadn't pierced his lung. So he decided to give the speech and wait until later for any medical treatment. He began by asking people to "be as quiet as possible." Then he added, "I don't know whether you fully understand that I have just been shot." He continued, "It takes more than that to kill a Bull Moose. But fortunately I had my manuscript, so you see I was going to make a long speech, and there is a bullet—there is where the bullet went through—and it probably saved me from it going into my heart. The bullet is in me now, so that I cannot make a very long speech, but I will try my best."

People also are often speaking literally when they say that a particular health book saved their life. If you have ridiculously high cholesterol, a book that helps you lower your bad and bring up your good may well save your life. And I'm sure all sorts of practical books have helped save lives: seamanship books that teach lost sailors how to navigate by the stars; wilderness survival books that tell you which mushrooms to avoid and how to scare off a hungry bear; and medical encyclopedias that help you determine when you are being a hypochondriac and when you need to rush yourself to an emergency room.

And then there are lifesaving books like *Just Mercy: A Story of Justice and Redemption* by Bryan Stevenson, a lawyer who is a hero in the fight against mass incarceration, racial inequality, and the death penalty; throughout the book, Stevenson returns to the story of his work on one death penalty case to help him illustrate American injustice. And there are novels like *The Confession* by John Grisham, the story of an innocent football hero with just four days to go before his execution. It's one of the most gripping thrillers I've ever read; it's also a devastating indictment of the death penalty—not only of its inhumanity, but also of how unequally it is applied and carried out. If capital punishment is ever finally abolished in the United States, the lives saved may in part be thanks to books like these.

Usually, however, when people say that this book or that book saved their life, they mean it in a spiritual sense. The book that saves a life may be the book that helps a reader realize she's not alone, or that gives her something to hope for, or that entertains her at a moment she desperately needs it, or reveals a path or paths she never knew existed.

I've heard from readers who grew up feeling as though no one else was like them in the world, or feeling that the world had no time or place for them—until a particular book spoke to them and showed them otherwise. *Bless Me, Ultima* by Rudolfo Anaya, *I Know Why the Caged Bird Sings* by Maya Angelou, *The Perks of Being a Wallflower* by Stephen Chbosky, *Love Medicine* by Louise Erdrich—these, among countless others, are books that readers feel helped save their lives. They may speak particularly strongly to readers who identify with one of the characters, but any book can speak to anyone. And it doesn't need to be memoir or traditional literary fiction or poetry; I've heard it said of books in every genre. Romance, science fiction, fantasy, narrative, graphic fiction, and nonfiction—all can save lives.

Has any book saved my life? I think it would be more accurate to say that books like James Baldwin's *Giovanni's Room* helped me choose my life. If it hadn't been for the books I read, I would have wound up with a life very different from the one I now lead. Books saved the life I have.

Reading Lolita in Tehran: A Memoir in Books by Azar Nafisi is a book about books changing lives, and it's a book that has saved lives. Nafisi was a teacher in Tehran, Iran, before, during, and after the Iranian revolution and the war against Iraq that followed Iraq's invasion of Iranian territory. The book begins with her describing a class she formed in 1995, after resigning her last teaching post in Iran. She invited seven of her students, all women, to come to her home to discuss literature every Thursday. As she describes it, "The theme of the class was the relationship between fiction and reality." Nafisi and her students read classic Persian works (*A Thousand and One Nights*) and Western literature (*Pride and Prejudice; Madame Bovary*). Eventually they read books by F. Scott Fitzgerald, Charlotte Brontë, and William James. And they did indeed read Vladimir Nabokov's novel *Lolita*. Nafisi is a scholar who had recently published a book on Nabokov, so it was natural that they would read his books.

Nafisi does realize that *Lolita* might seem a strange book to teach young women in postrevolutionary Iran. She writes: "I have asked you to imagine us, to imagine us in the act of reading *Lolita* in Tehran: a novel about a man who, in order to possess and captivate a twelve-year-old girl, indirectly causes the death of her mother, Charlotte, and keeps her as his little entrapped mistress for two years. Are you bewildered? Why *Lolita*? Why *Lolita* in Tehran?"

Soon, we learn the answer.

Nafisi explains to her students that *Lolita* is a book that goes "against the grain of all totalitarian perspectives." She talks with the young women about the powerful image of a "half-alive butterfly" in the novel and explores "the perverse intimacy of victim and jailer." But she is pulled up short one day by a question from one of her students, Mitra.

"Reaching for a pastry, Mitra says that something has been bothering her for some time. Why is it that stories like *Lolita* and *Madame Bovary*—stories that are so sad, so tragic—make us happy? Is it not sinful to feel pleasure when reading about something so terrible? Would we feel this way if we were to read about it in the newspapers or if it happened to us? If we were to write about our lives here in the Islamic Republic of Iran, should we make our readers happy?"

After a night spent pondering this, Nafisi thinks she has the answer and can't wait to share it with her students. She writes:

> Nabokov calls every great novel a fairy tale, I said. Well, I would agree. First, let me remind you that fairy tales abound with frightening witches who eat children and wicked stepmothers who poison their beautiful step-daughters and weak fathers who leave their children behind in forests. But the magic comes from the power of good, that force which tells us we need not give in to the limitations and restrictions imposed on us by McFate, as Nabokov called it.
>
> Every fairy tale offers the potential to surpass present limits, so in a sense the fairy tale offers you freedoms that reality denies. In all great works of fiction, regardless of

the grim reality they present, there is an affirmation of life against the transience of that life, an essential defiance. This affirmation lies in the way the author takes control of reality by retelling it in his own way, thus creating a new world. Every great work of art, I would declare pompously, is a celebration, an act of insubordination against the betrayals, horrors and infidelities of life. The perfection and beauty of form rebels against the ugliness and shabbiness of the subject matter. This is why we love *Madame Bovary* and cry for Emma, why we greedily read *Lolita* as our heart breaks for its small, vulgar, poetic and defiant orphaned heroine.

Reading Lolita in Tehran is, in many ways, a sad book itself, one in which the hand of McFate touches everyone. Nafisi describes how she lost, early in her life, any sense of security: one minute she is the daughter of a well-known politician, Tehran's youngest mayor, and going to school in Switzerland (albeit one she calls horrible); the next, she needs to return home, as her father is now jailed on trumped-up charges. For four years after that, the family was "told alternately that he was going to be killed or that he would be set free almost at once." And she also describes a brilliant academic career derailed for years by the punishing social and intellectual restrictions that followed the Iranian revolution. Nafisi is a target as a scholar of Western literature (particularly suspect for having received some of her education in Europe and America) and, more generally, as a woman. She is told she must abide by the "new rules," which include wearing a "head cover." She won't. So she loses her job. She writes in a letter to a friend that she has been made "irrelevant."

We meet, throughout the book, extraordinary young women who are persecuted, jailed, tortured, denied education, forced to marry, hounded. At one point, Nafisi writes of a slender young woman named Sanaz, who shows up late for one of the Thursday morning sessions. She is distraught and close to tears. Finally, after she sits down, with tea and water beside her, and after one of her fellow students attempts to lighten the mood with a joke, the others learn what has happened:

> Her story was familiar. A fortnight earlier, Sanaz and five of her girlfriends had gone for a two-day vacation by the Caspian Sea. On their first day, they had decided to visit her friend's fiancé in an adjoining villa. Sanaz kept emphasizing that they were all properly dressed, with their scarves and long robes. They were all sitting outside, in the garden: six girls and one boy. There were no alcoholic beverages in the house, no undesirable tapes or CDs. She seemed to be suggesting that if there had been, they might have deserved the treatment they received at the hands of the Revolutionary Guards.
>
> And then "they" came with their guns, the morality squads, surprising them by jumping over the low walls. They claimed to have received a report of illegal activities, and wanted to search the premises.

These young women were dressed appropriately, so they couldn't be criticized for their clothing; instead, one of the guards sarcastically criticized them for looking at the guards "with their Western attitudes." And even though the guards could find nothing amiss, the women were all taken to a special jail "for infractions in matters of morality."

For two days, they were kept there—in a "small, dark room" with a drug addict and prostitutes. "Despite their repeated requests, they were denied the right to call their parents. Apart from brief excursions to the rest room at appointed times, they left the room twice—the first time to be led to a hospital, where they were given virginity tests by a woman gynecologist, who had her students observe the examinations. Not satisfied with her verdict, the guards took them to a private clinic for a second check."

After a "summary trial," the girls were "forced to sign a document confessing to sins they had not committed and subjected to twenty-five lashes."

Because Sanaz was wearing a T-shirt under her robe, her jailers "jokingly suggested . . . she might not feel the pain, so they gave her more. For her, the physical pain had been more bearable than the indignity of the virginity tests and her self-loathing at having signed a forced confession." The final insult was that her parents now agreed with her brother that his sister had far too much freedom and should not be going on trips without male supervision.

Nafisi writes that she "cannot leave Sanaz and her story alone" and that she remembers "this incident just as I remember so many others from my life in Iran." They have, she writes, along with similar stories people have written or told to her after she left, become her own memories.

But just as those stories became her stories, so, too, did the stories she read and taught to the young women become their stories. *Lolita* and *Madame Bovary* became part of the lives of these young women, along with the Persian classics they read.

In the epilogue we learn what happened to some of the women. Several emigrated to Canada, America, and England. Three continued for some time to meet in Tehran, discussing Virginia Woolf and Milan Kundera and writing "about films, poetry and their own lives as women."

At the time of her writing, very little had changed in Iran. And yet it's clear that all of these young women's lives had changed—from the books they read and the discussions they had. Whether the books they read saved their lives or not, you would have to ask those women.

"Since then, however, there has been change in Iran," one scholar told me. "This is not because the regime is kinder and gentler, but because people—particularly women, the younger generation, and dedicated activists—constantly put pressure on the regime by contesting and transgressing their rules in public and private places."

There have been two waves of reform movements since the period Nafisi discusses. "Yes, they have fizzled out, or have been crushed," the scholar explained, "but they have had a significant impact on how people can live, read, and behave in private and public Iran today."

I've frequently seen *Reading Lolita in Tehran* on lists of books that can change or save your life. It's just one of those books. I recommend it to everyone I know, especially anyone who doubts that one teacher, one writer, one book can make a difference.

Reading Nafisi prompted me to search out other modern Iranian authors, leading me to Shahrnush Parsipur and Mahmoud Dowlatabadi, to name just two. They opened up new worlds to me, as Nafisi had done for her students. She also inspired me to read more Nabokov.

A book doesn't need to be thick enough to stop bullets. It doesn't need to lower your cholesterol. It doesn't even need to be a force for social good, though it's tremendous when it is. It just needs to be "an affirmation of life against the transience of that life, an essential defiance." It just needs to be the book you need when you need it.

"More More More," Said the Baby
Staying Satisfied

THERE'S A PICTURE BOOK by the beloved children's book author Vera B. Williams called *"More More More," Said the Baby*. It features three young children of different ages and shows how we can never get enough or give enough love. After Little Guy's father throws him into the air and catches him and kisses his belly button, Little Guy says, "More. More. More." And after Little Pumpkin's grandmother tastes each of her grandchild's toes, Little Pumpkin laughs and says, "More. More. More." And after Little Bird's mother gives her a kiss on each of her sleepy eyes, all Little Bird can utter is, "Mmm. Mmmm. Mmmm," as she falls asleep. In each pair, adult and child, the adult praises the child in word or song and holds the child close. It's a book overflowing with love, as represented by the words and the pictures, which are painted in vibrant colors: blues and purples and oranges and magenta. And as with all the great children's books—*Where the Wild Things Are* by Maurice Sendak or *Tar Beach* by Faith

Ringgold—this book delights children but also has uncanny resonance for adults.

Almost daily, the phrase " 'More, more, more' said the baby," pops into my head—though it's taken on a different meaning for me. That same quality in children that is so human and adorable becomes something of a horror in adults. In Vera B. Williams's wonderful world, adults give love and get it back multiplied many times over in the happiness of the children in their lives. But not all babies stop behaving like babies. The world is filled with people for whom enough attention, enough celebrity, enough wealth, enough power, enough adulation, is never enough. " 'More, more, more' said the baby." And when that baby is an adult, it's not at all cute.

When you read of global business leaders, with decades of achievement, being tripped up by an expense account run amok; or of politicians setting aside their principles to get an internship for a child or a sinecure for a spouse; or of beloved entertainers humiliating themselves on reality shows to stay in the limelight a few months more—then " 'More, more, more' said the baby" is the phrase that comes to mind.

But the examples don't need to be this extreme. There's the boss who again and again just has to take credit for an idea that is 95 percent due to the inspiration of one of her team members and 5 percent improved by her own tweak of it. (Buddhist business book author Marshall Goldsmith is withering when he writes about this managerial flaw in his book *What Got You Here Won't Get You There*.) Or the employee who dies a little every time a colleague is praised.

Or the friend who "had a *horrible* morning," solely because the person in front of him at Starbucks took a *crazy* long time to place her order.

This is not the justifiable rage of the dispossessed; this is the peevishness of those for whom enough is not enough.

Of course, it's plenty easy to decry this tendency in others. It's a little more painful and difficult to accept that the baby crying "More, more, more" is sometimes me.

I sometimes lie awake at night with alternating worries: Did I push too forcefully ahead at work, steamrolling someone else? Or did I let myself off the hook too easily, content to sit in the back when maybe I had something to say or add? And I expect that others might see my choices differently—charging me far more frequently with the crime of pushing too forcefully rather than neglecting to make myself heard.

The desire for more is certainly one of the things that moves mankind forward. Marie Curie didn't say after her first Nobel Prize, "Gee, I guess I can call it a day." In fact, she and her husband were so committed to their research that they didn't even go to fetch the Nobel. She continued soldiering away in her labs, discovering radium and polonium, among other things, and earning herself a second Nobel—becoming the first person ever to win two of them.

And Steve Jobs certainly could have relaxed (with money and reputation to spare) long before launching the iPhone and changing forever the world and what we do with our hands all day.

So how do we distinguish between the kind of "More,

more, more" that drives the world forward, and the kind that causes us to lose our way? And how do we know when it's time to press on—to demand, to insist, to persevere—and when it's time to ease up?

The answer is that we usually don't. History has very few elegant exits.

The most famous example from classical times of a person who was happy to relinquish the stage is the dictator Cincinnatus. According to the Roman historian Livy, Cincinnatus spent a mere two weeks and two days as absolute ruler of the Roman Republic. This allowed him enough time to make the changes that he thought needed to be made to protect the city of Rome and its patrician/republican system. He then voluntarily relinquished his absolute authority and retired to the countryside. George Washington was a big fan of Cincinnatus. There was actually nothing in the United States Constitution during Washington's time to keep him from continuing to run for office term after term after term; following the example of his idol, he voluntarily stepped aside after two.

But given that Cincinnatus was, at heart, a principled and honorable fellow, I find his example less startling than other, less celebrated ones. In *Lives*, Plutarch's dual biographies of celebrated Greeks and Romans, the author (who was writing in first century Greece) chronicled a few. Perhaps his oddest and most extreme case of a person deciding to step away from the public stage is the later Roman dictator Sulla. He took part in one of the ancient world's great civil wars and triumphed in it, marching an army into Rome to seize control in 82 BCE. He slaughtered his enemies and gave himself full powers as dictator. But then he used those powers to strengthen the constitutional government and stepped aside. Plutarch (as translated by Aubrey Stewart and George Long) wrote of him:

> Sulla indeed trusted so far to his good fortune rather than to his acts, that, though he had put many persons to death, and had made so many innovations and changes in the state, he laid down the dictatorship, and allowed the people to have the full control of the consular elections, without going near them, and all the while walking about in the Forum, and exposing himself to any one who might choose to call him to account, just like a private person.

Having relinquished all power, Sulla was able to spend time with his wife, his actor-boyfriend, and a louche assortment of dancers and lute players. He also set about writing his memoirs. Sulla was not a widely beloved fellow during his lifetime. Or after. But what makes his retirement so dramatic was that his ambition was so epic. He was someone who sought ever more until one day he decided simply to stop. One of the mysteries that has endured is what made him do that; what made him decide that the time had come to go from being the most powerful person in his world to a regular citizen.

It's far easier to give up something you never really wanted, as Cincinnatus did, than to relinquish something you've fought and campaigned for all your life. For me, Sulla may not be the more inspiring figure, but he's the more relevant one.

And for me, Plutarch's *Lives* will remain a book that helps me untangle the thorniest issues of our times: finding the line between more and enough.

But that's not the only reason to read it. There is no better soap opera in the history of history or literature. All of the television serials of our times from *Dallas* and *Dynasty*, with their wealthy oil clans, to *Empire* (note the title), chronicling the lives of a ruling family in the music industry, to *Game of Thrones*, with its weird warring kingdoms—all of these are heirs to Plutarch's *Lives*. You don't know infighting and betrayal until you've read the way that Plutarch chronicles the shenanigans behind the warriors and politicians who ruled ancient Rome and Greece. Plutarch tells stories in pairs—alternating Greeks and Romans, and pausing periodically to sum up the main similarities and differences he is trying to highlight. He is interested in telling and showing his readers who was perfidious and who was brave, who behaved with honor and who carried on in the opposite way. For the most part, though, the people who behaved badly are vastly more entertaining to read about than the noble ones. Plutarch was at his best chronicling the worst.

There are some things of which you can never have too much or give too much—like love. That's why I keep Vera B. Williams's *"More More More," Said the Baby* close at hand. But for most everything else, more can easily become too much. And that's why I keep Plutarch's *Lives* next to it.

A Journey Around My Room
Traveling

LIN YUTANG WAS a constant traveler. In *The Importance of Living*, he bemoaned the fact that traveling had once been a pleasure but now had become an industry. The problem was that people didn't really travel anymore. What they did was "false" travel.

According to Lin, there are three types of false travel. The first is to journey abroad with the idea of traveling to improve one's mind; Lin was of the belief that it's actually quite difficult to improve your mind. He ripped into "the institution of tourist guides, the most intolerable chattering kind of interfering busybodies" he could imagine. He wasn't particularly interested in who did what when, and couldn't understand why adults would subject themselves to being herded about and lectured at like schoolchildren. He was also dubious about the quality of information that most guides provide.

For Lin, the second type of false travel is to travel "for

conversation." That is, taking a trip so that you can bore your friends with stories of it afterward. The American humorist Robert Benchley, who wrote for *The New Yorker* from the mid-1920s until the 1940s, was also irked by this habit and had a great method for disarming it, based on the assumption that "very few travelers know anything more about the places they have visited than the names of one hotel, two points of interest, and perhaps one street. You can bluff them into insensibility by making up a name and asking them if they saw that when they were in Florence." He employs this method when "confronted by Mrs. Reetaly who has just returned from a frantic tour of Spain, southern France, and the Ritz Hotel, Paris." She brings up Toledo; he asks her if she "pushed on to Mastilejo," a town whose name he has made up on the spot. When she admits she didn't, he tells her Mastilejo is "Toledo multiplied by a hundred. Such mountains! Such coloring!" Soon they are onto the real town of Carcassonne. Benchley continues his strong offensive, inventing sights right and left, quizzing her as to whether she saw "the hole in the wall where Louis the Neurotic escaped from the Saracens" or "the stream where they found the sword and buckler of the Man with the Iron Abdomen." Before he can continue much longer, Mrs. Reetaly is beating a quick retreat, and that's the last Benchley needs to hear of her vacation.

Lin's rant against travel merely for conversation included his disapproving feelings on the topic of picture-taking. Lest we think it's a new thing to bemoan the fact that no one today can eat a meal before photographing it from every angle, Lin wrote about how he had seen "visitors at Hup'ao of Hangchow, a place famous for its tea and spring water, having their picture taken in the act of lifting tea cups to their lips. To be sure, it is a highly poetic sentiment to show friends a picture of themselves drinking tea at Hup'ao. The danger is that one spends less thought on the actual taste of the tea than on the photograph itself." He went on to note that "this sort of thing can become an obsession" and decried tourists so "busy with their cameras that have no time to look at the places themselves."

The third type of travel he despaired of and considered false is any trip undertaken by anyone who is interested in traveling according to any kind of schedule. "Bound by the clock and run by the calendar as he is at home, he is still bound by the clock and run by the calendar while abroad."

Lin proposed a *true* type of travel, the goal of which is to become "lost and unknown." In his eyes, the true traveler "is always a vagabond, with the joys, temptations, and sense of adventure of the vagabond." He writes, "The essence of travel is to have no duties, no fixed hours, no mail, no inquisitive neighbors, no receiving delegations, and no destination. A good traveler is one who does not know where he is going to, and a perfect traveler does not know where he came from."

It's often just when I think Lin is being his most flip that he surprises me. What he goes on to say is that the true traveler has no attachments, and therefore must have compassion for everyone. He quotes a Chinese nun: "Not to care for anybody in particular is to care for mankind in general." He argues for travel to strange cities and also for nature travel, urging his readers to "travel to see nothing and to see nobody, but the squirrels and muskrats and woodchucks and clouds and trees." He tells the story of an American woman taken by Chinese friends up a misty mountain. There is so much mist, nothing can be seen, and yet her friends make her climb ever higher. When they get to the peak, the only thing they can make out is "the outline of distant hills barely visible on the horizon." The American woman protests, "But there's nothing to see here." And her Chinese friends reply, "That's exactly the point. We come up here to see nothing."

In Lin's view, you must possess the capacity to open yourself to seeing what's in front of and around you all the time, not just when you are on a special trip. He gives us a sizable translation from a Chinese philosopher who expands on this, explaining that seeing the beauty and grace in the most majestic mountains means nothing if you can't see beauty and grace in "a little patch of water, a village, a bridge, a tree, a hedge, or a dog. . . ."

A travel book that takes this philosophy as far as it can go and then further is that remarkable little book beloved by both Machado de Assis and Lin Yutang: *A Journey Around My Room*. (I read it in a translation by Andrew Brown.) As I mentioned earlier, this book was written in 1790 by a young French officer named Xavier de Maistre, who had found himself in some trouble over a duel (illegal) and was sentenced to house arrest. In the centuries before ankle-monitoring bracelets and the like, the authorities relied on the honor of young noblemen to fulfill their sentences after they had misbehaved. De Maistre, then twenty-seven, was a man of honor and did, indeed, stay inside his Turin room for the full forty-two days the court had ordered. With nothing else to do, he wrote a guidebook to his room, visiting over the course of those weeks various bits of furniture, paintings, his bookshelf, letters he'd kept, and his own memory of a charming and slightly rakish life—albeit one studded with war and loss as well.

De Maistre makes a case for traveling around his room as the truest kind of travel—and also the most democratic type of travel that has or will ever exist.

"The pleasure you find in traveling around your room is safe from the restless jealousy of men; it is independent of the fickleness of fortune. After all, is there any person so unhappy, so abandoned, that he doesn't have a little den into which he can withdraw and hide away from everyone? Nothing more elaborate is needed for the journey."

His journey costs him nothing. He exclaims that this kind of travel will be "lauded and feted" by those who have modest amounts of wealth, but will be even more popular among the rich. He tells the reader why he thinks this is so: precisely because it doesn't cost anything. The rich are rich because they like to *save* money. He also points out that room travel is a great way for the sick to journey, just as it is for those who are scared of robbers, precipices, and quagmires.

Like all good travel writers, de Maistre begins his book by giving us the lay of the land and the route he intends to take:

My room is situated on the forty-fifth degree of latitude, according to the measurement of Father Beccaria; it stretches from east to west; it forms a long rectangle, thirty-six paces in circumference, if you hug the wall. My journey will, however, measure much more than this, as I will be crossing it frequently lengthwise, or else diagonally, without any rule or method. I will even follow a zigzag path, and I will trace out every possible geometrical trajectory if need be. I don't like people who have their itineraries and ideas so clearly sorted out that they say, "Today I'll make three visits, I'll write four letters, and I'll finish that book I started." My soul is so open to every kind of idea, taste and sentiment; it so avidly receives everything that presents itself! . . . And why would it turn down the pleasures that are scattered along life's difficult path?

This is just the kind of travel beloved by Lin Yutang.

De Maistre is a charming storyteller, and he also employs a small cast of characters to break the boredom—his manservant and his dog appear from time to time. And he has theories, lots of theories, including an odd riff on Plato: While Plato theorized that we are all comprised of our self and another, de Maistre believes we contain a soul and a beast, and that the two often work at cross-purposes.

At the same time, de Maistre is nothing if not indolent. Sometimes he can barely be bothered to leave one piece of furniture for another. Sometimes he travels around the room by sitting in an armchair, leaning back so that the front legs come a few inches off the floor, and then shimmying side to side so that the chair creeps forward. He's like a bored six-year-old.

But just when you think the book is nothing but a charming divertissement (such as when he urges his readers to decorate their beds with calming pink and white linens), or a parody of the great travel books of his age—works written by soldiers who had returned from years in Egypt, for example—there comes a surprise.

There's a chapter about a friend of his, a fellow soldier, who died not in battle but of illness in our author's arms in their winter quarters. He misses the friendship dreadfully, and one of the most moving passages in the book is the trip he makes across his room to his desk in order to visit his old friend's letters.

Another surprise comes when our traveler ponders people with more luxurious digs. It seems at first like other flip and offhand sections of the book. But then comes this passage:

And why would I bother to consider those who are in a more agreeable situation, when the world is swarming with people who are more unhappy than me? Instead of transporting myself in my imagination into that superb *casin*[villa], where so many beauties are eclipsed by young Eugénie, if I wish to consider myself happy, I need only pause awhile on the roads that lead there. A heap of unfortunate folk, lying half naked under the porches of those sumptuous apartments, seem on the point of expiring from cold and misery. What a sight! I wish this page of my book could be known throughout the world; I would like it to be known that, in this city—where everything breathes opulence—during the coldest winter nights, a host of wretches sleep out in the open, with only a boundary stone or the threshold of some palace on which to lay their heads.

Here you see a group of children huddling close together so as not to die of the cold. There it's a woman, shivering and voiceless to complain. The passers-by come and go, quite untouched by a sight to which they are used.

Just as many travel writers before and after have done, de Maistre brought light to the injustices he witnessed, though in this case they were literally on his doorstep. His point: you don't have to travel the world to see the ways we mistreat one another; it's as close as the street outside our windows.

But when he wants to be awakened to what is going on in the world far from his window, and learn more about the human condition, there is another destination in his room that he can visit—his bookshelf, which is filled mostly with novels and a few books of poetry. These take him out of his room while allowing him to stay in it, and expand his experiences a thousandfold. He writes, "As if my own troubles weren't enough, I also voluntarily share those of a thousand imaginary characters, and I feel them as vividly as my own."

The day finally comes when de Maistre is allowed to leave his home, but he describes that day as the one on which his true imprisonment, which is like being "shackled in chains," resumes: "The yoke of business is going to weigh down on me once again; I will no longer be able to take a single step that isn't traced out for me by propriety and duty."

It's only in his room, with his memories and books and his window, that he feels truly free.

After reading *A Journey Around My Room*, I vowed that I would take a trip to my room every few months, and these have been some of the happiest days I've spent. It's an incredible luxury to be home and not sick, to wake up with no agenda other than to wander around the apartment all day. I can lie on the sofa and look at the light as it plays across a glass table. Or see the way it catches on a cracked ceramic vase. I can play with the shells I've brought back from the beach. I can admire our hearty little African violet. And I can visit my books, flipping through this one and then that to light on a passage.

This only works if I remain totally unplugged. The rules for such a day are simple—no electronics at all (except for music).

I'm finding that on a slow, lazy day, when I'm a traveler in my own home, just about anything I touch is new to me, as I see it differently than I have before, but each object also brings back memories, as I recall how I came to have it. On these days I spend touring my apartment, I almost always visit the letters I've saved, especially those from David Baer, my friend who died when we were in our twenties. As de Maistre writes about the letters from *his* friend, "What an intense, melancholy pleasure it feels when my eyes run over the lines traced by someone who is no longer alive."

De Maistre's *A Journey Around My Room* was a huge success in his life. Years after he wrote the book, he decided to follow it with a companion volume, a sequel of sorts, *A Nocturnal Expedition Around My Room*. This is a shorter and more philosophical work. In it, he journeys to the stars, simply by staring out his window at the spectacular beauty of the night sky.

He writes that he understands that most people don't see the stars because they are sleeping when the stars are out. But what he can barely comprehend is why anyone awake and wandering around at night would forget to look up and marvel at them. His theory is that since people can see the sky so often, and all for free, they can't be bothered to look.

De Maistre writes (in a tone of righteous indignation) that if he were the sovereign of some country, "every night I would have the alarm bell rung, and I would oblige my subjects of every age, every sex and every condition to go to their windows and look at the stars."

But then he engages himself in an argument with Reason, who insists on exceptions to the decree. What if it's raining? Or too cold? Or there's a chill? And shouldn't the ill be exempt? And lovers, too?

All good points.

As for us, now, we live in a world that is largely without stars. The light pollution all around us, in every city around the globe, makes them hard to see. On most nights, you can't view them from a room in New York or Hong Kong or London. You can barely see them in many of the world's smaller cities and towns. You might have to go far into the country-side to see the full grandeur of the night sky.

But de Maistre's principal point remains unchanged. Even if the stars are obliterated by light, there are beautiful things to see all around us, and we can't be bothered. But it's not because we are ill, most of us. Or because it's too cold. Or because we are blind with love. Or even because we spend so much time looking at little screens. It's because we are often so busy and distracted and self-absorbed that we can't be bothered to see what is right in front of us, in our rooms, on our streets, in the air.

The fault is not in our stars—or in our screens—but in ourselves.

Death Be Not Proud
Praying

IT'S CURIOUS how much time I spend reading prayers, since I don't consider myself to be very religious. I look for them everywhere and keep in my knapsack a handsome red leather-bound book of prayers from my Episcopal high school. A favorite is one from the *Book of Common Prayer* that has us ask forgiveness for having "left undone those things we ought to have done and done those things that we ought not to have done." When I'm experiencing free-floating remorse I read that prayer. It's like a broad-spectrum antibiotic. It takes care of just about anything and everything.

My mind is especially open to prayer when I'm reading a book: it's quiet, attentive, focused. Not so much when I'm on the Web or flipping through a magazine. And while I do like books of prayers, I have discovered many of the prayers I like best in novels and works of nonfiction and collections of poetry.

One of the prayers I turn to most often comes from a book about a boy named Johnny Gunther.

For me, Johnny Gunther will always be seventeen, a contemporary, just a few years older than I was when I first met him in the pages of *Death Be Not Proud*, just a few years older than my boarding-school classmate Lee Harkins was when she died from Hodgkin's lymphoma. But Johnny wasn't our contemporary; he was my father's. Johnny was born in 1929, my dad in 1927. If Johnny were alive today, he would be eighty-seven, maybe with grandchildren the age he was when he first got a stiff neck that turned out to be something far worse: a brain tumor.

In *Death Be Not Proud*, his father, journalist and author John Gunther, chronicles the last fifteen months of his son's life. There is little of the life before: a speedy introductory chapter introduces you to this handsome young man with beautiful hands. And there are a few chapters after Johnny dies, which include some of his letters and his diary entries, and in which his mother writes about her devastating grief—the pain she gets from seeing things that her son loved or would have loved, and her regrets:

> I wish we had loved Johnny more when he was alive. Of course we loved Johnny very much. Johnny knew that. Everybody knew it. Loving Johnny more. What does it mean? What can it mean, now?
>
> Parents all over the earth who lost sons in the war have felt this kind of question, and sought an answer. To me, it means loving life more, being more aware of life, of one's fellow human beings, of the earth.

It means obliterating, in a curious but real way, the ideas of evil and hate and the enemy, and transmuting them, with the alchemy of suffering, into ideas of clarity and charity.

It means caring more and more about other people, at home and abroad, all over the earth. It means caring more about God.

Johnny Gunther and I had little in common when I first read his story. As noted, he wasn't of my generation; the war his mother refers to is World War II. His parents were divorced; mine weren't. He was passionate about chemistry and science; both subjects baffled me. But I still identified with him keenly. And I also had more than a little crush on him. That's part of the magic of the book—everyone I know who has read this book feels the same way about Johnny.

In one of those odd synchronies that keep happening to readers, I discovered on rereading *Death Be Not Proud* that young Johnny, at age ten, met Lin Yutang. John Gunther tells a story of his son approaching Dr. Lin, "the first Chinese he had ever met," at a lunch party and going right up to him to ask, "Is it true what my father says, that no Chinese ever eat cheese?" If Gunther was mortified, he doesn't say. But he does tell what happened next: "Dr. Lin ruined my authority as a parent by walking firmly to the buffet and putting a large piece of cheese in his mouth."

Death Be Not Proud has some light moments, but it is mostly a painful book. Gunther lays out the events of those last fifteen months as a great reporter would. The painful head shavings, the surgeries, the bandaging, the discovery of an ever-worsening prognosis, the miraculous months when Johnny defied all predictions and rallied—Gunther chronicles them all. Johnny is almost preternaturally brave. Reading this book, as a teen, I wanted to be like Johnny should I ever encounter anything like what he encountered. I was pretty sure I wouldn't be—but I wanted to try. Johnny is also curious, eager to know the whys and wherefores of every procedure, though his parents do frequently shield him from the worst news. Still, he's at heart a scientist—and he figures things out.

Johnny doesn't live long enough to go to Harvard, where he's been admitted. But he is able, though terribly ill, to attend his boarding-school graduation.

His father writes:

As each boy passed down the aisle, there was applause, perfunctory for some, pronounced for others. Gaines, Gillespie, Goodwin, Griffin, Gunther. Slowly, very slowly, Johnny stepped out of the mass of his fellows and trod by us, carefully keeping in the exact center of the long aisle, looking neither to the left nor the right, but straight ahead, fixedly, with the white bandage flashing in the light through the high windows, his chin up, carefully, not faltering, steady, but slowly, so very slowly. The applause began and then rose and the applause became a storm, as every single person in the old church became whipped up, tight and tense, to see if he would make it. The applause became a thunder, it rose and soared and banged, when Johnny finally reached the pulpit. Mr. Flynt carefully tried to put the diploma in his right hand, as planned. Firmly Johnny took it from right hand to left, as was proper, and while the whole audience rocked now with release from tension, and was still wildly, thunderously applauding, he passed around to the side and, not seeing us, reached his place among his friends.

When my own ghosts come, the images of friends I've lost young, Johnny Gunther joins them. I must confess that when I see him it's not as he really looked—it's in the image of an actor named Robby Benson who played him in a movie. But he's there all the same. His father was one of America's most famous authors and I don't think about him at all—I think about his son. John Gunther ensured that his child would have a kind of immortality he himself doesn't.

The book's epigraph is the John Donne poem from which Gunther took the title: "Death, be not proud, though some have called thee / Mighty and dreadful, for thou art not so." The poem famously ends with the couplet "One short sleep past, we wake eternally, / And Death shall be no more: Death, thou shalt die!"

Someone told me that if you want to know what a book is really about just read the last word. The last word of *Death Be Not Proud* comes from the chapter that Johnny's mother wrote. That word is "life."

But that's not the *last* last word. Gunther gives that to his son, who wrote, shortly after his diagnosis, a prayer. What made this particularly noteworthy, his father tells us, is that his son never prayed. Gunther speculates that Johnny's aversion to prayer may have stemmed from the fact that he so disliked going to chapel at his grade school and harbored considerable "resentment at having been obliged to spend a good deal of time listening to organized religious exhortation." So his mother, Frances, introduced him to all different kinds of prayers to counteract that early inculcation: "Hindu, Chinese, and so on, as well as Jewish and Christian. He was interested in all this, but it did not mean very much to him at first. Then she started him on Aldous Huxley's anthology of prayer, *The Perennial Philosophy*, and told him how intimate and very personal prayer could be. Once she suggested that if it should ever occur to him to think of a prayer himself, of his own special kind, he should tell her. So, very casually, with an 'Oh, by the way . . .' expression, he said, 'Speaking of prayers, I did think one up.' He recited it and only disclosed later that he had previously written it down and memorized it."

Unbeliever's Prayer

Almighty God
forgive me for my agnosticism;
For I shall try to keep it gentle, not cynical,
nor a bad influence

And O!
if Thou art truly in the heavens,
accept my gratitude
for all Thy gifts
and I shall try
to fight the good fight. Amen.

What the Living Do
Living

THE PRIMARY *reason* I first turn to any book is curiosity. I wonder what will be inside it. Or I wonder why someone I know and trust loves it. Or I wonder why everyone I know loathes it. Or I've read the cover copy and wonder how our heroine's life "will be changed forever" after she encounters whatever it is the flap-copy writer has said she will encounter. Or I wonder why this book remains on shelves hundreds of years after it was written, or why I've never heard of it before, or why an author I love has mentioned it on the radio, or why it caught my attention at a particular moment.

And my primary *emotion* at the start of any book is hope—hope that it will teach me something or delight me in some way. From the delightful books, I almost always learn something, even if it's just how to experience delight. That's a bonus. Good books often answer questions you didn't even know you wanted to ask.

Once, on a breezy day, I met a woman in a small bookstore after a reading. She looked to be somewhere in her sixties.

She told me that she had just lost her husband. She said she had never been a big nonfiction reader but that her husband had loved history books and biographies.

"In his last years, though, he was in too much pain to concentrate on reading," she told me. "He kept starting books but couldn't finish them. When he died, he left a big stack of books by his bed, all with bookmarks. Some of those books he had barely started. Others he'd almost read to the end." She paused and then continued, "After he died, I didn't know what to do. But then I figured it out. I decided to finish those books for him. I'm reading them, one at a time, start to finish. He couldn't, so I will."

Just because he was gone, she told me, his reading didn't need to go with him. She read those books because she loved him; she read because she still could; she read because it helped her remember him.

Books and people are bound together. I can't think about certain books and not about certain people, some living and some dead. The joy I've had from these books and from these people, and all I've learned from them, merge into one stream in my mind.

We can't do much for the people we've lost, but we can remember them and we can read for them: the books they loved, and books we think they might have chosen. Maybe the reading can help us answer the questions they would have asked us if they were still here to ask them. Maybe the reading can help us figure out how to honor their lives and continue their legacies. And maybe the reading itself can help us answer one of the biggest questions we can ask ourselves: Why are we here at all?

Every book we've read and everyone we've known, living and dead, is with us. We can call upon all of them. I was reminded of this when a friend told me I *had* to read a collection of poetry called *What the Living Do*. It's an extraordinary cycle of poems, published in 1998, by the American poet Marie Howe, related to the illness and death of a younger brother from AIDS.

One of the poems is called "My Dead Friends."

MY DEAD FRIENDS

I have begun,
when I'm weary and can't decide an answer to a bewildering question

to ask my dead friends for their opinion
and the answer is often immediate and clear.

Should I take the job? Move to the city? Should I try to conceive a child
in my middle age?

They stand in unison shaking their heads and smiling—whatever leads
to joy, they always answer,

to more life and less worry. I look into the vase where Billy's ashes were—
it's green in there, a green vase,

and I ask Billy if I should return the difficult phone call, and he says, yes.
Billy's already gone through the frightening door,

whatever he says I'll do.

A Final Word

THE BOOKS I've written about in this one are a small sampling of the works that have been my companions: books I've read, misread, reread, and recommended. I've neglected to mention most of my favorites. And I've yet to read many books that will surely join that list, as I don't yet know what they are. Some will be volumes written centuries ago, and some are being written right now.

I used to say that the greatest gift you could ever give anyone is a book. But I don't say that anymore because I no longer think it's true. I now say that a book is the second greatest gift. I've come to believe that the greatest gift you can give people is to take the time to talk with them about a book you've shared. A book is a great gift; the gift of your interest and attention is even greater.

Reading is a respite from the relentlessness of technology, but it's not only that. It's how I reset and recharge. It's how I escape, but it's also how I engage. And reading should spur further engagement.

When you read about injustice, you need to do something about it. Books have played a role in almost every one of the world's great civil and human rights movements, but only because people who read them decided to act. Reading brings with it responsibility.

In this way, some books have already helped change the world. Other books have the power to do so, even if they haven't quite yet. One of those, I believe, is *The Importance of Living*. That's part of the reason I keep returning to it.

The Importance of Living is about the need to slow down and enjoy life. And about the importance of books and reading. But it is ultimately an impassioned plea for reason and humanity. Lin Yutang urged us to appreciate poetry and literature not just as good things in and of themselves, but also because they encourage a kind of humanized thinking that he felt was essential for the survival of our race. Lin believed that hope for our world resides in people's adopting what he called the Spirit of Reasonableness, which he saw in the best of the Chinese traditions: "No one can be perfect; he can only aim at being a likable, reasonable human being."

Writing this book in 1937, Lin was keenly aware of the dangers on the horizon in both Europe and Asia, and he was eager to make one thing particularly clear. "Communism and Fascism are both products of the same mind," he warned in *The Importance of Living*. "Characteristic of both regimes and ideologies are, firstly, the sheer belief in force and power. . . ."

Lin taught me that I don't actually need a Ginsu-knife of a book. Nor, I suppose, do I really want one. In fact, the world tends to get into trouble when people claim that one particular book is the only book you need or should have, and especially when one group tries to force others to recognize their book as that one book.

Books remain one of the strongest bulwarks we have against tyranny—but only as long as people are free to read all different kinds of books, and only as long as they actually do so. The right to read whatever you want whenever you want is one of the fundamental rights that helps preserve all the other rights. It's a right we need to guard with unwavering diligence. But it's also a right we can guard with pleasure. Reading isn't just a strike against narrowness, mind control, and domination: It's one of the world's great joys.

How we live is no trivial matter. Racing around in a state of agitation and greed and envy isn't just wasting our lives; it's a symbol of much that is wrong with our world. And reading all different kinds of books is not simply reading all different kinds of books; it's a way of becoming more fully human and more humane.

When I read, I'm reminded to be more thoughtful about how I approach each day. And that's not just important for living: it's the least I can do for the dead.

I read to live. I read for life.

Acknowledgments

I am far more grateful than I can say to Sonny Mehta, for giving me the chance to write this book, for his comments and encouragement, and for his kindness. Also to Dan Frank, for his superb guidance and care, and to Betsy Sallee, who helped with a million and one things. And to Erinn Hartman, Kim Thornton Ingenito, Kate Runde, and Angie Venezia, who keep me happily busy and who always know the perfect thing to say and do. And to Paul Bogaards, Gabrielle Brooks, Carol Devine Carson, Robin Desser, Edward Kastenmeier, Chip Kidd, Stephanie Kloss, Nicholas Latimer, Cassandra Pappas, Victoria Pearson (including for the epigraph), Anne-Lise Spitzer, and Sean Yule. And to Chris Gillespie and the awesome Knopf sales team.

I'm equally blessed to have Two Roads as my UK publisher. Lisa Highton is a miracle: great friend, great publisher, and great drinking buddy. Thanks, too, to Fede Andornino.

I'm perpetually grateful to the remarkable team at Brockman Inc.: Max Brockman, John Brockman, Katinka Matson, Russell Weinberger, and Michael Healey.

In many ways, this book grew out of conversations with Alice Truax. She challenged me, coaxed me, and helped me at every turn throughout the entire process. Her contributions to this book and my life are enormous. There is no one better to have in your corner than Alice. She amazes me every time we talk.

Several friends read the manuscript at various stages. Marty Asher and Betsy Lerner gave me massive amounts of their time and genius. Lisa Queen is the person I turn to again and again when I need help writing, thinking about writing, or avoiding writing. She is one of the wisest people I know, and also one of the most generous.

Lin Yutang's youngest daughter, Hsiang Ju Lin, spoke with me for hours. She and her sister Lin Taiyi also allowed me to bring Lin Yutang's *The Importance of Living* back into print when I was at William Morrow.

Mimi Baer helped me with the section on her son David; Emily Harkins Filer shared wonderful stories about her daughter, Lee Harkins. I'm blessed to know them both.

The clever and resourceful Chloe Sarbib helped me with myriad tasks. Thanks, too, to Fred Courtright.

At work, I'm lucky to have an incredibly supportive boss, Andrew Weber, and terrific colleagues, including Kara Rota and Bryn Clark.

I'm also deeply blessed with wonderful friends. A few who were particularly helpful on this book were Tom Molner and Andy Brimmer, who continue to fortify me, amuse me, and house me during the summer; Molly O'Neil Frank, whose midlife calling to the chaplaincy inspired me; and Bill Reichblum, who has over decades introduced me to many of my favorite books (and beverages). And conversations with the following friends helped me on various chapters: Kedron Barrett, Rich Benjamin, Doris Cooper, Elisabeth Dyssegaard, Laurie Eustis, Jonathan Galassi, Emily Gould, Sara Holbrook Guggenheim, Hpoun, Zareen Jaffery, Walter Kaiser, Mollie Katzen, Larry Kramer, Jamie Lustberg, Bob Miller, Nahid Mozaffari, Marco Pasanella, Rebecca Robertson, Erika Robinson, David Shipley, the Tutorial, Will Winkelstein, and Naomi Wolf.

Some of the book was auditioned at Bob and Sally Edgar's dinner table. Bob was a spectacular teacher, and he and Sally are spectacular friends. I also want to thank my pals Rocco DiSpirito and Rick Brenders for helping me look after myself. And immense thanks to Josef Astor for the epic gifts of his friendship and photography.

I can never sufficiently thank my father, Doug Schwalbe, for all he has done for me, and also for so many great conversations over many decades. Apple's motto is "Think Different." My father is someone who has always done exactly that. And my mother is also present here on every page.

I owe unbounded thanks to my brother, Doug, and my sister, Nina, for their constant love and support. Also to Sally Girvin and Nancy Lorenz. And to my aunts and uncles, cousins, godchildren, niece Lucy, and nephews: Nicolas, Adrian, Milo, and Cy.

And then there's my husband, David Cheng. There are no words that can describe what he means to me. I could "count the ways," but I can't count that high.

Appendix

An alphabetical listing of the authors, books, plays, poems, stories, and journal articles discussed or mentioned in *Books for Living:*

Mitch Albom, *Tuesdays with Morrie*

Dante Alighieri, *The Divine Comedy*

Rudolfo Anaya, *Bless Me, Ultima*

Maya Angelou, *I Know Why the Caged Bird Sings*

Diane Arbus, *Diane Arbus: Revelations*

Joaquim Maria Machado de Assis, *Epitaph of a Small Winner (The Posthumous Memoirs of Brás Cubas)*

Jane Austen, *Pride and Prejudice*

Jane Austen and Seth Grahame-Smith, *Pride and Prejudice and Zombies*

James Baldwin, *Giovanni's Room; The Fire Next Time*

J. M. Barrie, *The Little White Bird; Peter Pan*

Joseph Beam

Robert Benchley

Rose Levy Beranbaum, *The Cake Bible*

The Bhagavad Gita

The Bible

Isabella Bird

Edward de Bono, *Lateral Thinking: An Introduction*
(first published as *The Use of Lateral Thinking*)

Boston Women's Health Book Collective, *Our Bodies, Ourselves*

John Boswell

Jane Bowles

Paul Bowles

Charlotte Brontë

Emily Brontë, *Wuthering Heights*

Rebecca Brown, *The Gifts of the Body*

Pearl S. Buck, *The Good Earth*

Anthony Burgess, *A Clockwork Orange*

Samuel Butler, *The Way of All Flesh*

Toby C. Campbell, M.D., "When Minutes Matter,"
The Journal of the American Medical Association
(*JAMA*) 314, no. 17.

Truman Capote

Miguel de Cervantes, *Don Quixote*

Chang Ch'ao

Bruce Chatwin

Stephen Chbosky, *The Perks of Being a Wallflower*

G. K. Chesterton, *What's Wrong with the World*

Lee Child, *Killing Floor*

Winston Churchill

John Ciardi, *Manner of Speaking; The Little That Is All:* "East Sixty-seventh Street" and "A Poem for Benn's Graduation from High School"; "Washing Your Feet"; *The Divine Comedy* (translation)

Paulo Coelho, *The Alchemist*

Suzanne Collins, *The Hunger Games* series

Laurie Colwin, *Home Cooking; More Home Cooking*

Confucius

e e cummings

Dianne Mott Davidson, *Sticks & Scones*

Patrick Dennis, *Auntie Mame*

Charles Dickens, *David Copperfield*

Isak Dinesen, "Babette's Feast"

Melvin Dixon

Hilda "H.D." Dolittle

John Donne, "Death Be Not Proud"

Rita Dove

Mahmoud Dowlatabadi

Arthur Conan Doyle

Charles Duhigg, *The Power of Habit*

Albert Einstein

Louise Erdrich, *Love Medicine*

Laura Esquivel, *Like Water for Chocolate*

Sebastian Faulks, *Birdsong*

Robert Ferro

F. Scott Fitzgerald

Gustave Flaubert, *Madame Bovary*

Gillian Flynn, *Gone Girl*

Ford Madox Ford, *The Good Soldier*

E. M. Forster

Robert Frost

William Golding, *Lord of the Flies*

Marshall Goldsmith, *What Got You Here Won't Get You There*

Henry Green

John Grisham, *The Confession*

Michael Grumley

John Gunther, *Death Be Not Proud*

Edward T. Hall, *The Hidden Dimension*

Paula Hawkins, *The Girl on the Train*

Essex Hemphill

Eugen Herrigel, *Zen in the Art of Archery*

James Hilton, *Goodbye, Mr. Chips*

S. E. Hinton, *The Outsiders*

Vyvyan Holland, *Son of Oscar Wilde*

Homer, *The Iliad; The Odyssey*

Vincent C. Horrigan and Raymond V. Schoder, *A Reading Course in Homeric Greek*

Marie Howe, *What The Living Do:* "My Dead Friends"

Robert Hughes, *The Fatal Shore*

Thomas Hughes, *Tom Brown's School Days*

Victor Hugo, *Les Misérables*

Aldous Huxley, *The Perennial Philosophy*

William Inge, *The Dark at the Top of the Stairs*

Christopher Isherwood, *A Single Man; Christopher and His Kind*

Arturo Islas

The Jākata (Stories of the Buddha's Former Births)

William James

Franz Kafka

Yasunari Kawabata

Marie Kondo, *The Life-Changing Magic of Tidying Up*

The Koran

Larry Kramer

Milan Kundera

Stephen E. Lahey, *John Wyclif*

Anne Lamott, *Bird by Bird; Traveling Mercies; Help, Thanks, Wow; Stitches*

John Lanchester, *The Debt to Pleasure*

Nigella Lawson, *Feast*

Bruce Lee, *Tao of Jeet Kune Do*

Stan Leventhal

Edna Lewis, *The Taste of Country Cooking*

Hsiang Ju Lin and Tsuifeng Lin, *Chinese Gastronomy*

Lin Yutang, *My Country and My People; The Importance of Living; Between Tears and Laughter*

Anne Morrow Lindbergh, *Listen! The Wind; Gift from the Sea*

Joan Lindsay, *Picnic at Hanging Rock*

Livy (Titus Livius)

Rosa Luxemburg

Thomas Mann, *Death in Venice*

Xavier de Maistre, *A Journey Around My Room; A Nocturnal Expedition Around My Room*

Daphne du Maurier, *Rebecca*

Mayo Clinic Family Health Book

Herman Melville, *Moby-Dick;* "Bartleby, the Scrivener: A Story of Wall Street"

Arthur Miller, *Death of a Salesman*

Rohinton Mistry, *A Fine Balance*

Paul Monette

Marianne Moore

Jan Morris

Toni Morrison, *Song of Solomon*

Mohammed Mrabet

Haruki Murakami, *A Wild Sheep Chase; The Wind-Up Bird Chronicle; Kafka on the Shore; What I Talk About When I Talk About Running; 1Q84*

Vladimir Nabokov, *Lolita*

Azar Nafisi, *Reading Lolita in Tehran*

Christopher Nolan, *Under the Eye of the Clock*

George Orwell, *1984*

Ruth Ozeki, *A Tale for the Time Being*

R. J. Palacio, *Wonder*

Shahrnush Parsipur

Walter Pater, *Marius the Epicurean*

Nathaniel Philbrick, *In the Heart of the Sea*

Robert M. Pirsig, *Zen and the Art of Motorcycle Maintenance*

Plato

Pliny the Younger

Plutarch, *Plutarch's Lives*

John Preston

Erich Maria Remarque

Faith Ringgold, *Tar Beach*

J. K. Rowling, *Harry Potter* series

John Ruskin

Vito Russo

Assotto Saint

Antoine de Saint-Exupéry, *The Little Prince*

Maurice Sendak, *Where the Wild Things Are*

William Shakespeare, *King Lear; Hamlet*

George Bernard Shaw, *Bernard Shaw: Complete Plays with Prefaces*

Randy Shilts

Samuel Smiles, *Self-Help (with Illustrations of Character and Content)*

Socrates

Andrew Solomon, *Far from the Tree*

Muriel Spark, *The Prime of Miss Jean Brodie*

Bryan Stevenson, *Just Mercy*

William Strunk Jr. and E. B. White, *The Elements of Style*

Jacqueline Susann, *Valley of the Dolls*

Sir Wilfred Thesiger

Henry David Thoreau, *Walden*

A Thousand and One Nights

Monique Truong, *The Book of Salt*

Mark Twain

John Updike

Gore Vidal, *The City and the Pillar*

Alice Waters

Alec Waugh, *The Loom of Youth*

Evelyn Waugh, *Brideshead Revisited*

Eudora Welty

E. B. White, *Stuart Little; Charlotte's Web; The Trumpet of the Swan; The Elements of Style* (with William Strunk Jr.); *Letters of E. B. White*

Oscar Wilde

Tennessee Williams

Vera B. Williams, *"More More More," Said the Baby*

Percival Christopher Wren, *Beau Geste*

Hanya Yanagihara, *A Little Life*

Yüan Chunglang

PERMISSIONS ACKNOWLEDGMENTS

Machado de Assis, excerpts from *Epitaph of a Small Winner*, translated by William L. Grossman. Copyright © 1952 by William Grossman. Reprinted by permission of Farrar, Straus & Giroux, LLC.

Rebecca Brown, excerpts from *The Gifts of the Body*. Copyright © 1994 by Rebecca Brown. Reprinted by permission of the author and her agents Harold Schmidt Literary Agency and HarperCollins Publishers.

John Ciardi, excerpts from "East Sixty-Seventh Street" and "A Poem for Benn's Graduation from High School" from *The Collected Poems*, edited by Edward M. Cifelli. Copyright © 1974 by John Ciardi. Reprinted with the permission of The Permissions Company, Inc., on behalf of the University of Arkansas Press, www.uapress.com. Excerpt from book jacket for John Ciardi, *The Little That Is All*. Reprinted with the permission of Rutgers University Press.

Xavier de Maistre, excerpts from *A Journey Around My Room*, translated by Andrew Brown. Copyright © 2013 by Andrew Brown. Reprinted with the permission of Alma Classics Ltd.

John Gunther, excerpts from *Death Be Not Proud*. Copyright © 1949 by John Gunther. Reprinted by permission of Jane Perry Gunther and HarperCollins Publishers.

Eugen Herrigel, excerpts from *Zen in the Art of Archery*, translated by R. F. C. Hull. Copyright © 1953 and renewed © 1981 by Pantheon Books, a division of Random House, Inc., and renewed 1981 by Random House, Inc. Used by permission of Pantheon Books, an imprint of the Knopf Doubleday Publishing Group, a division of Penguin Random House LLC. All rights reserved.

Marie Howe, "My Dead Friends," from *What the Living Do*. Copyright © 1998 by Marie Howe. Used by permission of W. W. Norton & Company, Inc.

A NOTE ABOUT THE AUTHOR

WILL SCHWALBE has worked in publishing; in digital media, as the founder and CEO of Cookstr.com; and as a journalist, writing for various publications, including the *New York Times* and the *South China Morning Post*. He is the author of *The End of Your Life Book Club* and coauthor, with David Shipley, of *Send: Why People Email So Badly and How to Do It Better*.

A NOTE ON THE TYPE

The text of this book was set in Van Dijck, a modern revival of a typeface attributed to the Dutch master punchcutter Christoffel van Dyck, c. 1606–69. The revival was produced by the Monotype Corporation in 1937–38 with the assistance, and perhaps over the objection, of the Dutch typographer Jan van Krimpen. Never in wide use, Monotype Van Dijck nonetheless has the familiar and comfortable qualities of the types of William Caslon, who used the original Van Dijck as the model for his famous type.

Typeset by Scribe,
Philadelphia, Pennsylvania

Printed and bound by Berryville Graphics,
Berryville, Virginia

Designed by Cassandra J. Pappas